Margaret Morris

Penguin Education

A Special Case?
Edited for the NUM by
John Hughes and Roy Moore

A Special Case?

Social Justice and the Miners
Edited for the NUM by
John Hughes and Roy Moore

Penguin Books

Penguin Books Ltd, Harmondsworth,
Middlesex, England
Penguin Books Inc., 7110 Ambassador Road,
Baltimore, Maryland 21207, USA
Penguin Books Australia Ltd,
Ringwood, Victoria, Australia

First published 1972
Copyright © NUM and contributors, 1972

Made and printed in Great Britain by
Hazell, Watson & Viney Ltd,
Aylesbury, Bucks
Set in Monotype Plantin

Contents

Note on Abbreviations

The following abbreviations occur in this book:

CBI	Confederation of British Industries
CEGB	Central Electricity Generating Board
CIHA	Coal Industry Housing Association
DHSS	Department of Health and Social Security
FIS	Family Income Supplement
ILO	International Labour Office
IMTA	Institute of Municipal Treasurers and Accountants
NBPI	National Board for Prices and Incomes
NCB	National Coal Board
NES	New Earnings Survey
NPLA	National Power Loading Agreement
NUM	National Union of Miners
OMS	Output per manshift
WPIS	Weekly-paid industrial staff

Preface

The miners did not stand alone. We found that in our struggle for industrial justice we had many friends in the ranks of organized labour and even more widely among the people of Britain. That support was vital, since the miners were confronted by a policy of wage restriction backed by the Government itself. People sensed the justice of our claim, and they sensed too the dangers of a Government response that initiated a power confrontation instead of weighing the case on its merits.

We owe it to those many people who rallied to our support to publish the substance of the miners' case to the Wilberforce Inquiry. In our case we demonstrated the force of reason. By contrast, the Government could not back up its power confrontation by rational argument; it could not lay claim to social justice. Social justice brought success to our claim, and our case strengthens the forces of social justice.

We present here not only our case, an edited form of the evidence to the Court, but also the response to it in the Wilberforce Inquiry Report. *The Times* commented:

The Wilberforce Report conceded almost all the miners' case. . . . It reads like a printed version of the arguments used by NUM leaders.

But we did not think of our case as presented solely to a tribunal of three men or to be weighed only by them. We thought of it as a case submitted to the people of Britain. Hence this book.

The miners did not stand for themselves alone. What made our struggle the most important one by any trade union in this generation was that we stood for the needs and concerns of millions more workers. We spoke for all the workers in the public sector who had found collective bargaining degenerating as their 'employers' became merely the mouthpiece of a rigid norm. We sought to put public-sector bargaining back into operation as a serious process concerned with the merits of the case. We knew that we had not been the only industrial group that had been frustrated when trying to draw attention to industrial injustice. For that reason, as part of our case, we invited Professor Clegg, with his exceptional understanding of the industrial-relations system, to argue for a more reasoned approach both to our case and to the 'special cases' of the future.

Not only that. We put as our priority the needs of the low-paid worker. We sought and achieved a settlement providing bigger increases for the lowest-paid than for our higher-paid workers. We brought the voice of low-paid workers to the Inquiry through miners' witnesses from the coalfields. We called in Michael Meacher, MP, the country's leading expert on the 'poverty trap' in which millions of workers are caught, to explain their dilemma.

This wider concern that we showed, at a time when we might have argued only in terms of our own narrowly defined interests, makes our case essential reading for the rest of the trade-union movement and for all those who seek a rational and constructive solution to the needs of Britain's workers.

When we put together our case for presentation to the Wilberforce Inquiry we found we had to set down a great deal in a very short space of time. We entrusted this task to the NUM's industrial-relations department, working in liaison with the staff from Ruskin College's Trade Union Research Unit who are editing the present publication. Somehow our small office staff managed to complete this task and produce a hundred copies of our full written evidence within three days, working round the clock. To them and to the many others who gave assistance and support, we would like to express our deep gratitude.

The case as presented in this book has been edited to simplify some of the detailed argument used, and to introduce some of the important questions and answers from the Wilberforce proceedings.

J. GORMLEY (President)
S. SCHOFIELD (Vice-President)
L. DALY (General Secretary)

Introduction

At the request of Lord Wilberforce the General Secretary of the National Union of Mineworkers, Lawrence Daly, opened the Court's proceedings.

For the first time in this dispute the mineworkers of this country find themselves able to speak out to men whom they hope will prove to have listened conscientiously and objectively to their case. We asked our employers for the opportunity of real collective bargaining. When we tried to argue our case with them we found we were confronted by men whose minds had been made up for them. They were men who had no power to settle. They had been instructed to keep within limits, which necessarily meant that they could not listen to a single one of our arguments. The men who gave them those instructions have not, in their turn, come forward to bargain with us.

In speaking to this Court of Inquiry we are also speaking to millions of people beyond these four walls. We are speaking to, we are appealing to, the conscience of the nation; we are appealing to the conscience above all of the working people of this country.

Many of these people have now got caught up in the effects of this dispute. The Government that has so disastrously denied us any channels of fair dealing, that has denied us any genuine process of conciliation, that same Government has now moved on towards a general lock-out of the working people of this country.

The Government has said that it has had to act now because of the effectiveness of our pickets. What it means is that it would have let this affair drag on even longer if we had not, through our picketing, brought forward the economic impact of the miners' strike. We are entitled to ask whether it would have been to the benefit of the coal industry of this country to have had this dispute drag on for several more weeks because we had not picketed. We ask the NCB, would that have improved the state of the pits or the Coal Board's finances? We ask our miners' wives, would that have helped to feed our children? And there need be no doubt that this appalling Government, the worst Government the miners have experienced in this century, would have done for weeks more what it did for the previous five weeks. It would have done nothing. It would have continued its futile, primitive nonsense of trying to create the suffering that might break men's wills.

Our pickets have done something more than hasten the course of this dispute. They have acted as ambassadors of the mining community in every city and port of this country. We have enjoyed in practical form, and with steadily growing effectiveness, the solidarity and support of the organized workers of this country. Instead of remaining isolated and alone beside our pits, we have built the unity of action and understanding that has been the immense positive feature of this strike. It is that and that alone that has forced the Government from the dictatorship that it has been imposing not just on miners but on all the workers of this country.

Those picket lines have been the one way of shortening this dispute and moving from Government dictation to a just settlement. When the industrial workers of Birmingham marched in their thousands to join our picket line they showed that we do not stand alone, and that the purpose of our picket lines is understood by the working people of this country.

I repeat. The NUM has throughout sought to bargain for a settlement. We are ready to do so today. We do not see the sittings of this Court as an impediment to such bargaining. But we can only bargain with those who have the industrial authority to bargain. We cannot bargain with those who have abdicated their industrial responsibility and who, having accepted a dictated pay ceiling themselves, seek then to impose it upon us.

We are the victims of the degeneration of free collective bargaining in face of Government coercion. We will be calling expert witnesses to comment on the inadequacies of the industrial-relations system of this country as it affects workers like ourselves, because we are conscious that the critical weaknesses of the collective-bargaining and industrial-conciliation systems as we have experienced them are not something peculiar to miners. These weaknesses have deeply affected virtually all the workers in the public sector in particular. Last year it was the Post Office workers; and before that the workers in electricity supply. The year before it was the dustmen and other local-authority workers. We are the end of a long line, and the industrial-relations system in which we are expected to operate has become less able to cope with our needs as public-sector workers.

Before embarking on the main body of the NUM evidence to the Court may we explain one thing. In view of the urgency of the situation we have not sought to burden the Court with the usual detailed blow-by-blow exposition of the chronology of events in this dispute. We have turned instead, directly, to the real issues, the real causes that have to be expressed.

1 The Years of Decline

By behaving out of character in a determined effort to improve his lot, the mineworker has discovered in 1972 that he has many distant admirers. A review of the past few years reveals that he has, to his credit, displayed unselfishness to his colleagues and loyalty to his industry. This may not have brought the material rewards which he needed, but it has placed him very high in the esteem of millions of people in this country.

He has displayed great patience and understanding in past years when others sought to persuade him that his demand for real improvements in his standard of living should be moderated in the national interest to keep a viable coal industry. Immediately following the Second World War, the Mineworkers' Union agreed to the Government's request for a low coal-pricing policy in the national interest. Regular Saturday working continued, also in the national interest. Meanwhile the nation, including coal's competitors, reaped the benefit and the mineworker lived less comfortably than he could have done had he exploited his strong position.

Up to 1958 the number of men employed in coalmining fluctuated around the 700,000 level, but then started on a decline which continued until 1970–71, when it settled at 287,200 for the annual average. Nineteen fifty-eight was the turning point in many respects. This is particularly true in respect of earnings. In the 1950s through to 1957, miners' weekly earnings were 25 per cent higher than those of workers in the manufacturing industries. Regular Saturday working finished, which for many meant a real cut in earnings at the very moment when future industrial prospects started to look uncertain.

Pit closures brought heavy redundancies. The possibility of

additional redundancies loomed as mechanization was introduced on an increasing scale. In 1957 approximately 5 per cent of
output was from mechanized faces compared with 92·2 per cent
in 1970–71.

The steep upward productivity trend started in 1957–8 from
an average of 25 cwt per man to 44·2 cwt in 1970–71. Observers
of the scene in and out of Parliament acknowledged the effort,
but the miner did not collect his just reward for his labour and
cooperation. Over the last decade, face output per manshift has
risen at an average annual rate of 5 per cent – considerably faster
than manufacturing industries where less spectacular performan-
ces have sometimes produced greater rewards for their workers.

No other industry has passed through a peaceful revolution
comparable to that which has taken place in mining since 1958.
New working methods were welcomed by the men and their
Union, even when the technical revolution removed many of the
higher-paid jobs and restricted earnings capability.

New working methods introduced new jobs. Many of these
required new skills, and consequently old wage structures became outdated. New ones were proposed and accepted, i.e. the
National Power Loading Agreement (NPLA) and the Third
National Daywage Structure. They were more appropriate to
the requirements of the labour force in modern mining and,
reinforced by a new Craft Structure, represented a commendable
attempt at rationalizing the industry's pay structure.

An element of redistribution of wages was introduced during
this rationalization, the Board and the Union justifying it on the
basis of a more even demand for effort from each workman than
in the past, and the need to provide a stable base upon which a
more realistic wage structure could be built. The miner has been
persuaded to greater effort by successive governments, and he
has responded. He has been crushed by government policies
which have obliterated whole mining communities in the national
interest (such as in Durham and parts of Wales) and he has
accepted that tragedy in a manner born from years of living and
working with imminent disaster. Many of those who survived
these calamities and worked on in the industry moved round the
country experiencing two or three further pit closures, wishing
in desperation for a stable situation.

Those who remained in the areas of fairly secure employment were naturally uncertain about the future of the industry and consequently inhibited in their approach on matters relating to pay and conditions. Therefore, approaches to the National Coal Board on pay questions were coloured by the anxiety of the Union and its members about future prospects and the need to preserve the maximum number of jobs in the industry.

The decline in the mineworker's earnings is attributable not only to this psychological pressure but also to the fact that the NUM and the NCB have steered the industry into a daywage system of wage payments. Consequently, unless regular overtime is available, the minimum rates quoted in the wage scales are also the maximum, with no production bonus incentives. This, we repeat, is a deliberate policy on the part of the NUM and the NCB. However, it was anticipated by the NUM that once the rationalization of the industry's wage structure had been completed, real progress would be made to restore the mineworker to a more favourable relative-earnings position. The decline in the relative earnings of mineworkers is severe when compared with a mere four years ago, but if the comparisons are extended back over fifteen years, the relative deterioration is one of over 25 per cent in weekly earnings. Only an increase in the scale of the Union's current claim would meet our needs. We are unable to find an equivalent example of a large group of workers in the British economy suffering anything like this decline in relative earnings. This unique factor is of great importance because it suggests that the general level of pay settlements elsewhere in the public sector at the present time should not be taken as a guide. To do so would perpetuate the decline that the mineworker has experienced.

As indicated previously, the decline is in some part due to the rationalization of the industry's wage structure, without compensatory increases in basic rates over the years to offset the loss of higher earnings opportunities which were there for some underground workers in the piecework system. The first national daywage structure was introduced in 1955, and the Union was committed to the extension of the daywage principle by Annual Conference decision. However, it was not until 1966 that the National Power Loading Agreement was brought in to cover workers on mechanized faces. This Agreement replaced the pit and district agreements which were in existence at that time, but it did not immediately introduce a national rate of pay. However, the Agreement carried a commitment that there would be one uniform national rate by 31 December 1971.

The Nottinghamshire District was rated second highest to Kent and it was agreed that it would be at the Nottinghamshire rate that uniformity would be achieved. The implication is obvious. Mineworkers doing the same jobs in other districts would have to achieve an equal rate of pay to workers in Nottinghamshire and Kent. To this extent the men cooperated in support of achieving the principle of one rate for the job wherever it is being performed. This is a concept alien to the traditions of mining communities, where local bargaining is the accepted practice and the local Union bargainers have considerable status. In 1966 the Nottinghamshire NPLA shift rate was 86s. 9d. and the lowest-paid districts, of which there were six, were on a shift rate of 75s. (see Table 1).

Table 1 **Increases in the National Power Loading Agreement Shift Rates since 1966**

| | 1966 | | 1970 | | January 1972 |
	s	d	s	d	£
Scotland	75	0	90	9	5
Northumberland	81	0	95	9	5
Durham	75	0	90	9	5
Yorkshire	82	6	97	1	5
Lancashire	84	5	98	8	5
Cumberland	75	0	90	8	5
North Wales	75	0	90	9	5
Nottinghamshire	86	9	100	0	5
North Derbyshire	84	5	98	8	5
Leicestershire	79	3	96	8	5
Cannock Chase	79	6	94	9	5
North Staffs	76	11	94	1	5
South Staffs and Shropshire	75	0	93	1	5
Warwickshire	83	2	97	9	5
South Wales	75	0	90	9	5
Kent	89	5	100	0	5
South Derbyshire	83	1	97	10	5

It may seem unlikely that an employer should seek the support of the Union in depressing the wage increases and wage levels for any section of its workers, but this in effect was the case. If the relative earnings for the whole industry were getting out of line it was even more acute for the Kent and Nottinghamshire NPLA workers. However, they accepted the position, though as higher-paid districts, which were also high production areas, they could have used their strong bargaining position. Thus, the Union's policy to narrow the wage gap between the highest and lowest-paid of its manual worker members was accepted.

The introduction of the NPLA did not complete the process of getting the industry on to a daywage system. There were still some 70,000 piece- and task-workers whose rates of pay were decided by local bargaining. Informal talks between the Union and the NCB started in 1968 with a view to bringing in a Third National Daywage Structure into which these 70,000 would be assimilated. The important factor in the Union's approach to these negotiations is the courage it displayed in controlling wage drift, despite the tradition of local negotiations. An important drawback to the proposals was that the upper qualifying limit for the increases imposed a wage freeze on some workers who were performing very skilled mining work. Many mineworkers argued that the skilled and demanding nature of their job meant that it could not be undertaken on a daywage basis. However, the Third National Daywage Structure was completed and introduced in June 1971, which meant that the whole labour force would be covered by the daywage system. Three grades were introduced and the rate for each grade was an approximate average of the rates being paid in the country for that type of work. For some there would be increases; for others, a definite wage reduction as they came on to the new structure. The degree of movement for Grade A employees is illustrated in Figure 1 (page 19).

All this was done as part of the Union's strategy in the process of rationalizing the industry's wage structure. The objectives were:

1. To narrow the wage gap between the highest and lowest-paid in the industry.

2. To establish national rates of pay for each job in the industry.

3. To arrive at a set of job values which were appropriate to the work being performed in modern mining.

4. To establish wage levels which gave a reasonable standard of living and adequate work initiatives, and presented an attractive prospect to new recruits.

The Union not only agreed to limit the pay increases of certain sections but effectively reduced the earnings of many in order to raise the wages of the lower grades. The assumption was that by cooperating in this way there would eventually be a stage at which those who had sacrificed real wages or earnings prospects would be part of a general move forward to realistic wage levels.

Members of the Court (Lord Wilberforce, the Chairman, and John Garnett) had difficulty in accepting the implications of the Figure and questioned Lawrence Daly (Secretary of the NUM).

CHAIRMAN: Is that right, Mr Daly, that people on the right – the 'pit-props' as I can call them – were all brought up to the new level?

DALY: Yes.

CHAIRMAN: But is it equally true that the people on the left were brought down?

DALY: Yes, in actual cash rates they were brought down.

GARNETT: And they actually lost money?

DALY: Oh, yes, net cash was taken from them, admittedly on the basis of a joint agreement between the Union and the Coal Board.

Figure 1 Third National Daywage Structure – Great Britain (excluding Kent)
The figure shows the effect of the introduction of the Third National Daywage Structure on rates of pay per shift. The central line represents the new rate to which previous rates were subordinated. The blocks to the right of the central line indicate the percentage of employees whose rates of pay per shift were increased by particular amounts. To the left of the central line are the percentages of workers whose pay per shift was reduced by particular amounts. In all such cases a worker would only retain his former higher rate as long as he remained in the same job at the same face

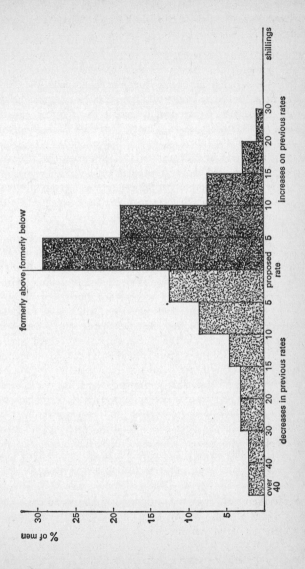

Laurance Hunter, a member of the Court of Inquiry, questioned Lawrence Daly on some of the points raised in this chapter.

HUNTER: From 1966 right down to 1971 you were working towards a long-term plan in terms of an overall wages structure, and this was something which involved some degree of sacrifice on the part of some workers, and the Union recognized in going into this that there would have to be sacrifices, but the workers were prepared to go along with this. You said in your statement that you had recognized that when this process had come to an end, and it came to an end at the end of December 1971, you would then be expecting or anticipating a reappraisal of the whole position of the mineworkers. . . . I am interested in the processes which were involved here and whether the policy change was very sudden.

DALY: The position is that it has been a long-standing policy agreed between the Coal Board and the Union to seek to eliminate as far as we can – it is not completely eliminated yet but we have gone a long way towards it – the local bargaining piece-rate system. This is in the interests of trying to establish the same rate for the same job irrespective of which mine in Britain it is done in. We think that it is a fair thing to do; it has been a long-standing policy of the Union and it was decided upon as far back as 1946. But we have found it difficult, of course, because of the complicated wages system in the industry, to move rapidly towards nationally uniform rates. It has taken many years, partly because of the complication of the local wage-rates system and also partly, to some extent, because there has been an understandable resistance on the part of some of our membership to this change because it has, in fact, meant not only that areas which I have already mentioned, like Nottingham and Kent, and others with relatively high pay, have had to advance with wage increases lower than the lower-paid coalfields which kept them well below the rate of increase in the cost of living. It has also meant for thousands of our members an actual cash reduction in earnings, some of them to the extent not of shillings but pounds per week during a period of inflation, and we have had to carry our members with us and have

conference after conference and meetings in the coalfields. It
has taken a considerable time to achieve our aim but even
where the membership have disagreed with it, in the main
they have cooperated and accepted the sacrifices involved in
the hope that more money can be made available for those
who are lower paid.

It is not our view that this should simply be done by robbing
Peter to pay Paul and there is no other industry in the country
where the members of the union in majority would agree to a
policy of this kind. I think we are unique in this respect. What
we did expect was the stabilization of the industry on the basis
of a fuel policy which would give the coal industry a proper
share of the energy market and provide stability of employment. We brought pressure on governments to do so, with no
great degree of success, and secondly we made it clear with
continuous representations to successive governments that we
did not expect that the whole of this could be done out of the
pockets of the men themselves. We demanded repeatedly a
capital reconstruction of the industry because the industry was
carrying debts that arose from the fact that we had huge
borrowings from the Exchequer in the 1950s, expecting that
the coal industry would be of the size of two hundred and fifty
million instead of its present size of one hundred and forty
million tons. I do not want to argue this here in detail,* but we
certainly did anticipate this, and that is why we brought pressure to bear on governments for a capital reconstruction which
we did not sufficiently achieve. We did get one in 1965 but it
was not big enough to overcome the debt with which the Coal
Board is faced.

*Lawrence Daly went on later to develop the points he had been
making in reply to Laurance Hunter.*

DALY: I would not like it to be thought that, although the mine-
    workers signed an agreement in 1966 to establish by gradual
    process a national uniform rate, which would be the level
    reached at 31 December 1971 for power-loading men in the

* The arguments are developed in chapter 5 (Eds.).

Nottinghamshire coalfields, our members or ourselves were particularly happy about it. We certainly did support the leadership of the Union and the majority of the membership in the principle of moving towards national uniform rates.

For obvious reasons many thousands of men in coalfields like Nottingham, who knew they were going to experience actual, and in many cases very substantial, net reductions in their cash wages, were opposed to this and it was not without great difficulty that this became the official policy in terms of the National Power Loading Agreement as we now understand it. It had been preceded in Scotland and Durham by divisional day-rate power-loading agreements and to a certain extent the Scottish agreement was taken as the model. While we had the main parts of our membership agreeing to the principle, we were most unhappy about the rate of movement towards a nationally uniform rate. The Coal Board's argument was that the money necessary to bring such numbers of men up to the Nottingham rate could simply not be found before completing the process by 31 December 1971. It was to be a gradual step-by-step process and, indeed, part of the difficulty this year, or from the commencement of negotiations in September last year, arises from the fact that despite our protests the National Coal Board insisted, in the settlement of November 1970, that there would be no move towards parity. They gave the same increase across the board for every power-loading worker and that left the National Coal Board this year with a much bigger problem to carry to find the money to achieve parity, which has now been achieved by 1 January 1972.

This was not a very happy agreement for us, not in principle, but in the speed and in the way, in many cases, in which we moved. It was an unhappy experience for many men who went from contract work to power-loading agreement with very substantial reductions in wages. While we re-emphasize the fact that we support the principle of nationally uniform rates, I would also like to say that you must not think that because we have got beyond 31 December 1971 the problem is solved. It is not. We still have many thousands of men who have not yet moved on to the nationally agreed rates in the third national structure agreement and who will in the coming months, in many cases, be moving on to whatever the third structure agreed rate will be, which will be the same as that decided for the power-loading-agreement men. These men can see that unless there is a reasonable increase, and in this sense our proposal for the men at the coal face for at least from £30 to £35 is a most modest one, they are going to be in the position of moving on to jobs at which they will again be – not all of them, there are numbers who will come up – going down in actual cash wages when they go on to whatever rate is established. So the problem is still with us to some extent, although admittedly to a lesser extent than it was during the period 1967–70.

That is why, in order to persuade our men to accept the Power Loading Agreement, and even more recently, last year, to persuade our men where there were objections and we had special meetings (for example, in a coalfield like Nottingham), we had to point out to them that, even though thousands of them had made sacrifices, and more of them would sacrifice, if we stuck to the principle of nationally uniform rates being introduced by 1 January 1972 we could assure them that, since we were now on one national, uniform rate system, we would then make a united effort to lift up the wages levels substantially so that the plateau of wages on to which they would personally fall would be a bit higher, so that the fall for them would not be as substantial as it would otherwise be. This was an additional reason why we have argued the case very strongly for the men at the lower end of the scale. We do want a reduction in the differential between the underground men elsewhere and the men at the face, but it is still extremely important that the face rate ought to be established at the figure we have suggested.

2 The Arithmetic of Declining Earnings

The relative decline in earnings

It is possible, using official statistics, to indicate with considerable accuracy the relative decline in miners' earnings over recent years. The most recent figures available to us are the New Earnings Survey data for April 1971. The official earnings figures from the then six-monthly Enquiry of April 1967 show the kind of relativities that had stabilized during the earlier 1960s. Expressed in pounds and new pence, the figures for manual men in coalmining as compared with all manufacturing industries are shown in Table 2.

Table 2 **Average weekly earnings, manual men, April 1967**

	£ p	Index (manufacturing = 100)
All manufacturing	21 13	100
Coalmining	22 60	107

The New Earnings Survey information so far available for April 1971 refers to the manual workers covered by the agreement between the NCB and the NUM (see Table 3). The figures relate to men who worked during the whole or part of a particular pay-week. This maintains, as far as possible, comparability with the 1967 figures.* Both 1967 and 1971 data exclude allowances in kind.

* Difficulties associated with this are discussed in an editorial note on page 145 (Eds.).

Table 3 **Average weekly earnings, manual men, April 1971**

	£ p	Index (manufacturing = 100)
All manufacturing	30 20	100
Coalmining	28 10	93

The decline in miners' earnings has thus brought them down from 107 per cent to only 93 per cent of the manufacturing average in just four years. Indeed, April 1971 was a time of exceptional depression in manufacturing, and this sharply curtailed overtime hours. Consequently, the 1971 manufacturing figure is clearly lower than it would have been if there had been the same level of activity as in 1967. In other words, the 1971 comparison to some extent conceals an even greater deterioration in the relative position of mineworkers, because the manufacturing figure was temporarily lower than normal.

An indication of this bias is that between April 1970 and April 1971, average weekly hours worked in mining increased from 40·3 to 41·2, whilst in manufacturing they fell from 45·4 to 44·4. The effect of this was to give a boost of at least 3 per cent to miners' weekly earnings (allowing for overtime premia), and to reduce manufacturing weekly earnings by at least as much.

It is useful at this stage to distinguish between underground and surface workers in coalmining.

Underground workers

Comparisons over a longer period, based on earnings figures excluding those whose pay was affected by absence, confirm the conclusion that underground miners' pay has fallen relatively behind other workers'. According to the Ministry of Labour's October 1960 survey, underground workers' average earnings were over 110 per cent of the average in manufacturing. By 1971 they were down to 97 per cent of the manufacturing figure, according to the Department of Employment's April 1971 New Earnings Survey. The increase over the ten and a half years for underground workers was less than 77 per cent; in manufacturing overall the increase was 101 per cent.

In April 1971 average earnings of underground workers, at £30.20, were already below the manufacturing average of £31.10, still excluding those whose pay was affected by absence. It is, therefore, not the case that lower earnings of surface workers were pulling down the overall coalmining industry's earnings below the average level in manufacturing. Underground workers themselves were at a clear disadvantage.

Surface workers

The plight of surface workers, often themselves long-serving underground workers, is sharply illuminated by their earnings figures. In April 1971, 24·6 per cent of them earned less than £20 gross a week, which is twice the comparable figure of 11·5 per cent for semi-skilled workers overall; 49·6 per cent of them earned less than £25, which is five times the comparable proportion in manufacturing overall; and 73·2 per cent of them earned less than £30. In other words, and including only those who worked a full week, one in every four surface workers had gross earnings of less than £20; two in every four got less than £25; and three in every four got less than £30. Surface workers' earnings were thus consistently below the earnings of semi-skilled workers elsewhere, all through the earnings range.

The moral should be quite clear. Earnings in coalmining have deteriorated in relation to those of workers elsewhere to a considerable degree. Moreover, *all* mining employees are at these disadvantages. Many surface workers are low-paid by any standards, despite the last agreement. Surface workers are less well rewarded than semi-skilled workers elsewhere, and their colleagues working below ground are paid less than employees of manufacturing industries.

Finally, we need to quantify the degree of the decline in miners' earnings in money. It is easier to grasp the extent of the gap that has opened up in earnings terms between the miner's current pay and his earlier position if this is expressed in cash terms. The calculation is as follows:

In April 1971 the average full-time manual man working in manufacturing earned £30.20.

On a seasonally adjusted basis the most recent figures show average earnings in manufacturing rising at 12 per cent a year, or 1 per cent a month. (This is likely to accelerate once output begins to rise more rapidly.) Thus, by early 1972 we can estimate that average earnings of men in manufacturing will be about £33.

If the miner were to restore the slight earnings lead over the manufacturing worker that he held in the earlier 1960s, he would need weekly earnings about 7 per cent above the manufacturing average, i.e. just over £35.

In April 1971 average earnings were £28.10. The increases in certain areas, due to the NPLA, at the beginning of 1972 may raise this earnings figure to about £29.20.

Consequently, it would require an increase in weekly earnings of about £6.50 to restore to the miner the earnings status he enjoyed a few years ago. Given the relationship between wage rates in the industry and weekly earnings (to which we shall be drawing attention later), this would mean a wage increase averaging over £5 a week.

The absolute decline in earnings

So far we have been discussing the decline in *relative* terms of our members' earnings, in comparison with other industries. We now wish to confront the Court with the fact that miners have also suffered an *absolute* decline in real living standards over the past few years.

Our members have suffered in two ways from inflation. Firstly, they have moved into earnings ranges carrying greater tax liability; and, secondly, they have seen the purchasing power of their take-home pay reduced by rising prices. Moreover, the removal of reduced rates of tax, and the lowering of the 'threshold' level of earnings at which standard rate becomes payable, have both served to increase the degree to which tax cuts into our members' incomes.

Even if we go back as far as 1960, the effect of rising prices can be seen to have absorbed almost all the increased earnings gained by miners. In October 1960 average earnings of underground workers in mining were equivalent to £17.10 in decimal currency (Ministry of Labour 1960 Earnings Survey). The comparable average earnings figure, excluding those whose pay was affected by absence, from the 1971 New Earnings Survey (Department of Employment) was £30.20. This increase in earnings of just under 77 per cent was almost entirely absorbed by a rise in prices over the same ten-and-a-half-years period of just under 60 per cent. The increase in gross earnings at constant prices was thus only approximately 10·5 per cent, or less than 1 per cent per annum. Over the same period average earnings in manufacturing industries rose from £15.47 to £31.10, an increase of 101 per cent. This rate of increase gave manufacturing workers a real increase of nearly 26 per cent – twice as great as that which occurred in coal-mining.

As direct taxes were an increasing burden during these years, the deepening effect on the real disposable income of the average miner was greater still than that indicated by direct comparison with the retail price index.*

The effect of higher tax burdens can be illustrated by the fact that in 1965 the 'threshold' level of earnings at which standard rate was payable was 77 per cent of average earnings in mining for the married man without children. By 1971 it was down to only 41 per cent of miners' average earnings (New Earnings Survey basis). The corresponding figures for the married man with two children were 107 per cent in 1965, down to only 67 per cent in 1971.

It should be emphasized that the actual impact of taxation on real standards is greater than indicated, since we have not taken into consideration increased national insurance contributions, nor the cut-off points for means-tested benefit of various kinds introduced by this Government.†

Finally, we invite you to consider the special case of the face worker, and to compare the negotiated increases in the National Power Loading Agreement since 1966 with rising retail prices. The increases in the NPLA have already been laid out in Table 1 (see page 16) and are reproduced in Table 4 in index form at January 1972, based upon 1966 = 100.

* We have since been able to apply the findings of Table 9 in chapter 10 to the movement in miners' average earnings. The implication is that average take-home pay of miners has fallen, in real terms, by approximately 5 per cent over the period under consideration (1960–71) (Eds.).
† These points are developed in chapter 10 (Eds.).

Table 4

Area	Increase in rate 1966– January 1972	Decline in pay rate at constant (1966) prices
	%	%
Scotland	33·3	− 1·8
Northumberland	23·4	− 9·1
Durham	33·3	− 1·8
Yorkshire	21·2	−10·7
Lancashire	18·5	−12·7
Cumberland	33·3	− 1·8
North Wales	33·3	− 1·8
Nottinghamshire	15·3	−15·0
North Derbyshire	18·5	−12·7
Leicestershire	26·1	− 7·0
Cannock Chase	25·8	− 7·3
North Staffs	30·0	− 4·2
South Staffs and Shropshire	33·3	− 1·8
Warwickshire	20·3	−11·3
South Wales	33·3	− 1·8
Kent	11·7	−17·7
South Derbyshire	20·4	−11·2

The right-hand column shows that due to an increase in retail prices between 1966 and December 1971 of 35·7 per cent every single area has suffered a decrease in terms of constant prices. In no area has the increase in NPLA negotiated rates kept up with the increase in the retail price index.

No face worker has been able to keep up with rising prices on the basis of NPLA rates. The increasing incidence of income tax during the period, as already indicated, ate further still into the face workers' pay standards.

The attempts of Derek Ezra (Chairman of the NCB) to fault the NUM's presentation met strong rebuffs from Lawrence Daly, and helpful observations from Lord Wilberforce.

EZRA: I would like to refer to Table 3 on page 25, which shows that the earnings in coalmining in April 1971, were £28.10

compared with £30.20 in manufacturing industry. I would like to ask whether Mr Daly has taken into account the benefits in kind which are peculiar to the coalmining industry? In our estimation, those amount to £2.30, that is the cost to the Coal Board. Of course, if these benefits in kind were not made available to the members of the National Union of Mineworkers, they would cost them a good deal more, and I would like to know whether those have been taken into account in this computation?

DALY: When I made references, as I have done in the last two or three weeks, to your salary of £20,000 per year, I was by no means taking into account, either for you or the other members of the Coal Board, the various 'perks' that you receive on your job. The same with mining: these figures vary; there are thousands of members who do not qualify for concessionary coal, the vast majority do not qualify for cheap rents, many of them live in CIHA houses where the rent charged is the same as the rent charged by the local authority for similar accommodation, and for those who do have cheap rents they are generally nineteenth-century housing for which no one would expect to be paying much more than a few shillings in these days. So these are not taken into account, in the same way as they are not taken into account when we quote the figures for the other industries.

CHAIRMAN: Would this be right, Mr Daly, that you have not put them in on Table 3 on page 25, but you also have not put them in, have you, on Table 2 on page 24?

DALY: That is true.

CHAIRMAN: So the comparison might perhaps be rather the same: if you add it in one, you have to add it in the other. Is not that right?

DALY: That is right, Sir; and we have indicated that on Table 2 on page 24.

CHAIRMAN: But as a matter of fact the answer is that the concessionary payments and so on, the £2, is not in on either page?

DALY: Yes, this is true.

EZRA: I wish just to make an observation, my Lord. Would the Union agree that it is a fair observation for us to say that normally in the process of wage negotiations it is really not feasible to take into account such elements as tax deductions

as affecting particular categories of workers? These things are
determined by external factors particularly, in an industry such
as ours?

DALY: Normally one does not particularly mention this factor,
but we have reached the stage where the Government has set up
a Court of Inquiry so that the nation can find out everything
that is involved which has led to the present dispute and,
whether we like it or not, tax-rate changes and changes in the
ways in which means-tested benefits are applied over the recent
period must be taken into account if we are going to look at the
miners' real disposable income; this is the position.

3 Earnings and Pay Rates: The Special Case of Mining

There is no doubt that one of the obstacles to an adequate settlement of pay demands for miners has been the confusion over the relationship between pay rates and earnings in mining as against other industries.

The situation can be put in simple terms as follows. Pay rates are a far more important determinant of total earnings in mining than in other productive industries. Consequently, if mineworkers' pay rates are held down to a level near those of other groups of industrial workers this, in fact, ensures that miners' earnings fall badly behind. If, in earnings terms, miners are to secure a level of earnings compared with other workers that reasonably reflects the special features of their working conditions, then this requires a considerably higher level of pay rates – one well above the pay rates prevalent in most production industries.

The New Earnings Survey analysis of the 'make-up of pay' is not yet available for April 1971. However, the data for April 1970 are sufficiently reliable as an indicator of the situation. The Survey analyses the percentage of total gross earnings accounted for by basic pay and by other categories such as overtime, payment by results, etc. (The material is to be found in the *Department of Employment Gazette*, December 1970.)

In the case of full-time, manual men the overall position for 'All Index of Production Industries' is that only 67 per cent of total earnings are accounted for by basic pay. By contrast, for coalminers the figure is 79 per cent of total earnings accounted for by basic pay. Thus, for the miner to secure no more than the same total earnings as the worker in production industry, the miner's basic pay would need to be about 18 per cent higher than the basic pay of the average manual man employed in production industries.

This is not due to the fact that overtime constitutes any less important a part of the gross earnings of the miner than it does of other workers. In 1970 the Earnings Survey found that overtime constituted 16 per cent of the total earnings of men manual workers. For coalminers the figure was then 14 per cent. But the average hours per week of miners recorded in the 1970 Survey were 40·3; by the time of the 1971 Survey this had risen to 41·2 hours.

The main difference in the make-up of pay was, of course, the minor role played by payment by results in miners' earnings. At the time of the 1970 Survey the three categories of shift and other premium payments, payment by results, and bonus, accounted for 15 per cent of the total pay of the average manual man working in production industries (the figure is 18 per cent – even higher – in manufacturing) compared with only 5 per cent in mining. This latter figure is likely to be diminished further.

In other words, the general extension of the NPLA has decisively altered the relation between pay rates and earnings. The new comparison that might justifiably be made is with those high controlled time rates that have been established in a number of major firms with the extension of systems of measured daywork. The coal-face worker ought increasingly to be compared with, say, the workers on production lines in the car industry, where the hourly rates established under measured daywork and equivalent systems exceed £1 a hour in many cases. The comparison with traditional time rates is highly misleading.

Meanwhile, the figures that are already available from the 1971 Earnings Survey demonstrates that many miners working a full week unaffected by absence are securing gross earnings little more than the basic pay rate. The Survey showed that 10 per cent of adult miners working a full week had gross earnings less than £20. This is, of course, before deductions and taxation.

It is important to set out in detail how recent is the change in the composition of miners' earnings. In Table 5 the composition of the total earnings bill in mining is compared with that for manufacturing industries in 1968 and 1970:

Table 5

	Coalmining		All manufacturing industries	
	September 1968 %	April 1970 %	September 1968 %	April 1970 %
Basic pay	69·0	79·2	62·3	65·7
Overtime	12·2	13·8	16·3	15·7
Shift premia	1·1	1·1	3·3	4·0
Payment by results	11·5	2·3	13·2	9·9
Bonus	1·8	2·3	2·3	3·8

There are several interesting features here. First and foremost is the sharply increased significance, within total earnings, of basic pay in coalmining. This increase, from 69 per cent to over 79 per cent, means that comparison with other industries' pay on the basis of wage rates is quite inappropriate. The increase in the proportion of basic pay to total earnings in manufacturing was by contrast much less significant. It follows from this that basic wage rates would need to have increased considerably faster than rates elsewhere if miners were not to suffer a relative decline in their earnings position. This faster increase has not materialized, and consequently the relative decline has continued.

It is of course the development of the new wage system that cuts out the opportunities for increased earnings through incentive-based payments. Payment by results and bonus payments fell only 1·8 per cent from 15·5 per cent to 13·7 per cent in manufacturing; in coalmining the decline was from 13·3 per cent to 4·6 per cent. Incentive-based payments were thus by 1970 three times more significant in manufacturing than in coalmining.

There is extensive shift working in mining but it is very inadequately recognized in pay. The only allowance payable to mineworkers is that for certain workers for hours worked between 8.00 p.m. and 6.00 a.m. at the rate of 2½p per hour. The New Earnings Survey showed for 1970 that one quarter of the manual labour force in coalmining was in receipt of such payments. Shift payments in mining have remained static at only 1·1 per cent of total earnings. In manufacturing they have increased from three times to nearly four times this proportion. Comparison with another public corporation (steel) shows that shift payments have increased from five to five-and-a-half times the mining proportion.

For all of the above reasons, the miner has found himself at a fundamental disadvantage compared with workers elsewhere. In such circumstances overtime appears as the only way of enhancing his earnings. This is particularly so for the surface worker, as this April 1970 breakdown illustrates:

Table 6

	Underground %	Surface %
Basic pay	82·1	71·9
Overtime	10·1	22·6
Shift	1·1	1·5
Payment by results	3·0	0·8
Bonus	2·3	2·2

The surface workers' reliance on overtime is illustrated by the fact that between one-quarter and one-fifth of their total earnings is in such form. The underground worker is even more dependent on basic pay, however, in that this comprises over 82 per cent of total earnings. There are few industries where basic pay counts for a higher percentage of total earnings than it does in coalmining.

Our comparisons with other pay structures have been with manufacturing. There is an additional point to be made about public-sector pay. In many other parts of the public sector the change in the relation between pay rates and earnings has been the exact opposite of that in mining. Thus, in electricity supply, in the gas and water industries, in local-authority and hospital-service manual work, there has been a rapid extension both of 'lead-in' payments and of incentive-pay systems. This means that in these industries basic pay rates account for a *diminishing* proportion of earnings. The direction in which bargaining has gone in these other public-sector industries has been one which sought increased earnings through elements in the pay system besides basic rates.

Why are we emphasizing this? Because particularly in the most recent period since 1968 there has been a dramatic change in our pay structures. Incentive-pay elements have been removed. Never in his history has the miner been so dependent on basic rates for his earnings. Consequently, it is entirely fraudulent to put forward crude figures of miners' basic rates and those of other industries, as if these showed the true situation. This is even more obvious if the comparison is with other pay rates in the public sector, where an increased element of incentive pay is being introduced.

From 1968 onwards, in other words, if miners were to hope to maintain their relative position in earnings terms, their basic rates should have been advanced much more rapidly than was the case in other industries. That did not happen. This is how industrial injustice comes about.

Laurance Hunter asked Lawrence Daly whether the new pay structure amounted to measured daywork.

DALY: We have not tended to call it measured daywork, but, generally speaking, we have moved on to the power-loading agreement system, and that is responsible for about 94 per cent of the face output. The management sits down with the Union and tries to reach agreement on measuring the task which is expected to be performed by a team in a given shift. The element of the piece-rate system has virtually disappeared, so it is in effect measured daywork.

HUNTER: They are not continuing standards. The standards are set for a particular shift.

DALY: They vary because of geological conditions.

William Campbell Adamson, Director-General of the Confederation of British Industries, was obliged to accept the validity of the arguments in this chapter when questioned by John Hughes of the Trade Union Research Unit.

CAMPBELL ADAMSON: The only comparison I can use, not being in the industry, is the comparison between what the last offer would have given to the low-paid, and where the miners would have stood in the relative table. Both those things would bring them a very great deal above what many of my members in private industry are paid for those things.

HUGHES: Can I just say on this that I imagine you know that when we talk about the mining industry we are talking about an industry where earnings are primarily determined by pay rates? I do not think that is true, is it, of engineering?

CAMPBELL ADAMSON: 'Engineering', to my mind, is not a term that you can use; it is too diverse.

HUGHES: Could we say it is true of British industry in general?

CAMPBELL ADAMSON: There are quite large parts of it where it is true, and it will probably be more true as the situation goes on.

HUGHES: Could I quote you, then, the latest NES figure, that less than 70 per cent of earnings in industry generally are made up from basic rates?

CAMPBELL ADAMSON: Well, I accept the figure, if that is the figure.

HUGHES: So that we are not comparing like with like if we compare pay rates in the mining industry and pay rates in other industries?

CAMPBELL ADAMSON: I think you have got to compare earnings with earnings.

HUGHES: Thank you.

4 Productivity Proceeds and Earnings

We have explained the decline in the earnings and consequently the standard of living of our members. This is in striking contrast to the leap in productivity and the proceeds from the sale of coal.

In recent years the coal industry has secured rapid increases in productivity and an even faster increase in proceeds. This performance has not been matched by an equivalent advance in earnings, or in the real living standards of miners. This mismatch is particularly evident for coal-face workers.

'Face OMS' has risen rapidly over the last decade, at an average pace of 5 per cent a year or more. This is a faster increase than that secured in manufacturing industry. However, it may be argued that this rate of productivity advance was particularly due to the technological shift to fully mechanized face work. It therefore seems more appropriate to concentrate on more recent years, when the transition to mechanized faces has been largely completed. What emerges, however, is an even faster rate of productivity growth. From 1967–8 to 1970–71, OMS on mechanized faces rose by 20 per cent (or an average rate of about 6 per cent a year).

The NCB has made recent statements to the effect that on a mechanized face there is something in the region of £250,000 of equipment, all of which requires skilful manipulation and attention. The mineworker – always a craftsman – learned new skills as machines replaced men on the coal face and reduced the opportunities for progression to higher-paid jobs. He adopted no Luddite attitude but, as the record shows, put the machine to work with devastating results. Men cooperating with management and working with the machine lifted the coalmining industry to the top of the productivity league (league tables appear to be fashionable).

The 'overall' productivity performance is a good one (despite the fact that mining is a 'diminishing returns' industry), as Figure 2 indicates (page 40). Over the last decade the advance has been as fast, or faster, than in manufacturing industry. From 1967–8 to 1970–71 it was 13 per cent (again faster than manufacturing productivity was advancing).

Consequently, the appropriate assumption that the NCB should be making about the *trend rate* of productivity advance should be (overall) something of the order of 4 per cent a year. It should not take a short period of temporarily slower productivity advance as an indication of trend.

As proceeds per ton have been rising in recent years (from £4·93 in 1967–8 to £5·84 in 1970–71) the rise in proceeds per manshift has been even more pronounced. For each manshift on mechanized faces, proceeds increased by 41 per cent between 1967–8 and 1970–71. Overall, proceeds per manshift rose by some 35 per cent in the same period of three years. Given the further price increase at the end of the 1970–71 financial year, it is possible to estimate the further increase in proceeds per ton so far during 1971–2. From the index of wholesale prices, and what is so far known about productivity, it appears that proceeds per ton are about 16 per cent or over £0·90 up on the previous year. In consequence, proceeds per manshift 'overall' are probably between 55 per cent and 60 per cent higher in the current financial year than they were four years ago. None of this advance – either in 'real' terms or in money terms – is fully reflected in miners' earnings. The comparison is particularly adverse in the case of face workers. The NCB statistics show that cash earnings of face workers per manshift rose only 17 per cent in the three years from 1967–8 to 1970–71. This was considerably less than the average for all miners, and was a slower increase than the rise in the index of retail prices. Thus, a productivity rise of 20 per cent in three years on mechanized faces went hand in hand with an absolute fall in the earnings after adjusting for retail price increases.

The deterioration in earnings is not the full price that the miner may pay in extracting the maximum production from the

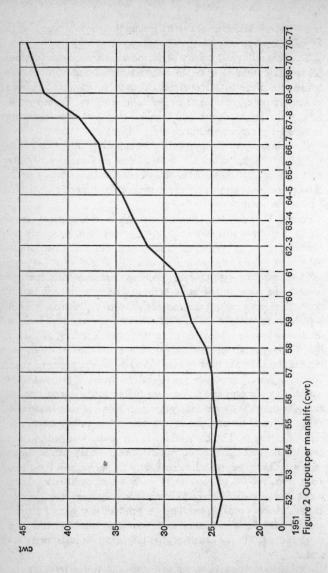

Figure 2 Output per manshift (cwt)

machine and himself in difficult conditions. It is in those conditions that the awful price of human suffering is paid and these surely demand consideration since they are unique to the mining industry. The simple fact is that the miner, with his very considerable physical and technical skills, must challenge the dangers inherent in the mining process and also those introduced by mechanization, electrification and explosives. And the sad fact is that the task is so formidable and complicated that he cannot always succeed. In the fiscal year 1970–71, coalmining claimed the lives of ninety-two miners, and 598 others received serious reportable injuries. The number of new cases of diseases in coal mines for 1970 totalled 3153. This figure excludes new cases of pneumoconiosis but includes such diseases as dermatitis, beat hand, beat knee, beat elbow, inflammation of the wrist, and nystagmus. Pneumoconiosis is of special significance. There were 773 new cases of this lung disease reported in 1970; and it is pertinent to note the comment made by H M Chief Inspector of Mines and Quarries in his Report for 1969 and 1970:

there is little comfort to be drawn from the figures of recent years and it is apparent that widespread mechanization has slowed down the decline in pneumoconiosis. Dust-suppression measures have not kept pace with production techniques and if the risk of an increase in the prevalence of pneumoconiosis is to be reduced in years to come a determined effort is now necessary to restore the balance in favour of dust suppression.

Laurance Hunter asked Lawrence Daly about the reasons for recent lower productivity:

HUNTER: You do yourselves comment on the short period of temporarily slower productivity advance. I take it you were referring there to the very slow change in productivity in 1969–70 and 1970–71. Would you like to comment on this or try to offer some explanation for the slow rate of advance, coming as it did after two years of very high advances?

DALY: First of all, it was obvious that we could not possibly maintain the same rate of increase in productivity that came about when there was a heavy pit-closure programme and manpower was being transferred into and concentrating on more modern

s.c. – 3

coal mines which were more productive. Secondly, there was sooner or later bound to be some decline in the gains from the actual mechanization programme at the coal face. Thirdly – and I think this will be of particular interest to the Court of Inquiry – we were told last year by the Board (this is on record in the minutes of the Coal Industrial National Council) that, thanks to our cooperation in improving the attendance of miners at work compared with the previous year, there was an improvement of 2 per cent. Because of the response in terms of recruitment, they considered this was largely due or at least partly due to the fact that we had to squeeze from the Coal Board the increase of £3 at the coal face that we got the year before. Due to improved recruitment and attendance and the fact that management were not able to put all these men on to production work at the coal face, the number of manshifts on work other than production work, work underground (i.e. transporting the coal, for example, from the coal face to the bottom of the pit shaft) and the number of manshifts worked there, the ratio of these to productive face jobs had risen. Consequently the divisor into the total global production became greater and the theoretical rate of increase in output per manshift came down to zero. This in no way can be put at the door of the miners, of course, who were in fact being congratulated for improving the attendance record. These are the factors. But, nevertheless, we are also discussing, and have been for a long time now with the Board, ways and means of improving production still further. For example, there are some places already where experimentation is going on in the mechanization of the drivage of underground roadways; and there is also a great deal of work being done jointly by the Union and the Board to eliminate what we call outbye delays in the transport system, etc. We think that the Board, on the basis of the work we are doing, should take a less pessimistic view of what further increases in productivity can be achieved.

John Garnett asked Mr Daly for his views on future productivity possibilities.

GARNETT: May I return to the productivity argument. I wanted to be clear from the Union side that the kinds of growth in productivity talked about by the Coal Board are the kinds of thing you think – if we could get the will right and get the co-operation right – could be achieved. We have heard of 4–5 per cent per year increase?

DALY: We think it may be possible, but the unique feature about the mining industry is the geological conditions and the uncertainties, even when there is sufficient research made of both a physical and a theoretical nature; very often the plan goes awry, as we know from many experiences. Notably, for example, the Beavercotes colliery up in Nottingham, and years back, if I take an example from my own coalfield, the disaster at Glenrothes colliery in Fife, which lost £30 million and produced virtually nothing but sand and water. We could quote many, many other examples. With the best will in the world, one can make an estimate to improve productivity by two or three hundredweight in a year, and in an industry of our kind one cannot with certainty say that such a forecast will be correct. Therefore, what we have indicated is, while we are not averse to speaking about productivity deals, and certainly all the time are involved with the Board in trying to improve efficiency and output, nevertheless we cannot say to our members that if they accept such a generalized proposal for a productivity deal, they will in fact reap any benefit. That is a very uncertain position in which to place our membership. I have already indicated that Lord Robens, not very long before he retired from the Chairmanship of the Board, said the Board had looked at something like twenty-one different schemes and none of them could be described as fair and practical at the same time. Years before that, the Union itself employed a firm of private consultants, at considerable cost and by decision of our conference, to examine the possibility of a national incentive scheme. They came up with a reply that it just was not fair or practicable.

That has not precluded us from keeping talking about the thing. There is no good in pretending that both sides sitting here with a line that anybody is satisfied can work. There are no details which have been put forward whatsoever.

GARNETT: I was not asking the pros and cons of a productivity scheme. What I was asking you was that if the will is right and, of course, geological factors apart – these are beyond the power of man, obviously, and are not in this discussion – is it within their ability and gifts and willingness – in your own words as you used them in your evidence, where you say 'men giving of their best to their work' – for that situation to be achieved? Do you see any reason why we cannot get this 4–5 per cent a year increase in production?

DALY: I certainly would not commit myself specifically to a 4 or 5 per cent increase in productivity. The Board itself was asked by the Select Committee on Nationalized Industry in 1969 to give their forecast of the rate per annum of productivity and they gave a figure of 10 per cent per annum, which we said was over-optimistic and proved to be drastically over-optimistic. Certainly, if you asked the question, the will is there on the part of the members of our Union to do everything in their power to produce a steady increase in productivity.

GORMLEY*: May I make a comment? If you are just asking the simple question, is there potential for output to be improved as a result of the machines which we now have working in the pits, the answer is inevitably 'yes'. We think there is scope. It's the ability for everybody to get the thing organized properly and see it is all geared together. To argue whether that productivity can be turned into a wages deal is something totally different. I hope you are not going to try and implicate anything in that direction. We have sat with the Board and agreed to set up a sub-committee at all levels to discuss the ways and means of increasing the production of coal from any machine in every pit in which it is at all possible. We feel there is a bit of leeway to make up. To one question, the answer is 'yes', but for wages, it is just not as easy as that.

* Joe Gormley is President of the NUM.

5 The Top-Heavy Debt Structure of the NCB

There is no doubt that, up to now, one of the barriers to a rational consideration of mineworkers' pay and conditions has been the debt structure of the Coal Board. That debt structure has become increasingly irrational, and has operated so as to prevent a sensible economic and financial strategy being carried out for the industry.

This helps to explain an extraordinary discrepancy. On the one hand we have the immense deterioration in the pay position of mineworkers – both in relative terms and for some groups also in terms of falling real living standards – and on the other the tremendous improvement in labour productivity in the last decade. As we have shown, productivity improvement is based not simply on equipment, but on the positive cooperation of the labour force (new working systems, flexibility, transfers of workers, in many places new shift systems, new pay structures, etc.). So there cannot be an industry anywhere in the country that offers such a sharp contrast between the trend of pay and the trend of productivity and labour effort.

It might also be said that there is not another industry in the country that is burdened to anything like the same extent with what is literally deadweight debt. This debt operates parasitically to drain away the surpluses of the industry's operations. It imposes itself as a prior charge carrying forward the debt payments that represent pits long since closed. This debt, based on capital assets that are long since dead, is imposed as a prior charge squeezing out the human needs of the living. Deadweight debt comes first; respect for the human needs of the industry's workers come a bad second. Each time the NUM begins to bargain it is confronted by the same story – the story of this phoney accounting, this artificial financial position.

If you study the Coal Board accounts you will find that each year the operating surplus of the Coal Board has to reach nearly £100 million for the Board's finances to 'break even'. Despite the rapid contraction of the industry we have an increasing provision for depreciation. How much of that is genuine? How much represents provision now for 'premature obsolescence', that is, for further contraction that may take place in the future? Thus, the accounts carry both the burden of the past – the debt is still there while the pits have been closed – and the burden of the future (the depreciation provision stepped up now because of the risk of future closures).

It is true that there was a modest concentration of the capital structure and some write-off of debt as one of the early acts of the Labour Government in 1965. This reorganization of the debt structure of the NCB operated so as to reduce sharply (in the financial year 1965–6) the interest payable. Interest payable (net) fell from £42·7 million in 1964–5 to £25 million in 1965–6. Subsequently, a somewhat artificial requirement to make an additional depreciation provision (nominally for 'replacement cost' purposes) was dropped. Thus, the accounts showed a direct benefit from the relief of some debt and a nominal one from a change from one arbitrary figure of depreciation to a lower one.

But since the last capital write-off a number of major changes have taken place:

1. Annual coal consumption has fallen by about forty million tons, and continues to fall. Consequently, fixed capital charges have to be borne on a diminished sales volume (i.e. increased capital charges per ton).

2. This fall has been partly due to the rapid development of natural gas, which was not foreseen at the time of the last capital reconstruction.

3. Additional borrowings by the NCB have been at high interest rates (averaging over 7 per cent). Consequently the interest payments as a prior charge on the accounts have risen rapidly.

4. In consequence, by 1970–71 interest payments per ton were

already higher (at 24p) than before the capital reconstruction. Depreciation provision is also rapidly increasing per ton.

5. After the capital reconstruction, net assets considerably exceeded the liability in terms of loans from the Secretary of State. By 1970–71 these reserves were eliminated as fixed assets diminished rapidly (mainly reflecting pit closures) and indebtedness increased. By 1970–71 loans from the Secretary of State exceeded net assets.

Perhaps the most straightforward statistic to show how much need there is for a write-off of the burden of debt is one that is not itself financial. We refer simply to the figures for pit closures since 1965 – that is *after* the last capital reconstruction. They are as follows:

Table 7 **Pit closures since capital reconstruction**

1965–6	52
1966–7	46
1967–8	51
1968–9	55
1969–70	19
1970–71	6
	229 including 1965–6
Total	177 excluding 1965–6

Thus Table 7 shows that from 1965 through to 1969 pits were being closed at a rate of about one a week. The pits were closed, but the debt stayed round our necks. Indeed, because of replacing old debt at low interest rates by renewed borrowing at high interest rates, it grew worse.

In saying that the slate should be wiped clean, that the debt should be written off, we are not asking for special treatment for the mining industry. We are asking for some of the better financial sense that has been displayed by governments in dealing with other industries. For instance, in recent years, very large sums indeed have been extended to private industry as direct subsidy (some of this to market rivals of the NCB such as the oil industry). Despite the massive problems of adjustment that the coal industry had to face, in the four years 1967 to 1970 current-account subsidies totalled only £57 million. Employment premiums to manufacturing industry in the same years totalled £635 million. (Had the NCB been given the 'regional employment premium' it would have added about £40 million to Coal Board income in those years.) To take a public-sector example, in the same years subsidies to transport undertakings on current account totalled £634 million. Thus, subsidies to manufacturing and transport were well over twenty times as great as the subsidies extended to the coal industry.

On capital account, the NCB has received minimal help since the write-off in 1965. In the four years 1967–70 nearly £1700 million in direct subsidy were handed out to manufacturing industry as investment grants (only a minute amount went to the NCB and then only on activities *other than* coal production). During the same years the NCB was having to finance its investment by borrowing at high interest rates, as already noted. Since the NCB received its partial capital write-off over £2000 million has been written off the debt of other nationalized industries. This figure (from the National Income Blue Book) is *before* the recently announced decision to write off a further £350 million of debt from the British Steel Corporation.*

It is worth looking at the Steel Corporation's capital write-off in more detail, partly because it is so recent (the Bill to give effect to it was only introduced into the House of Commons in December last) and partly because it points a direct moral. The Bill is intended to set up a reserve fund which can be used to offset existing and expected losses this year and next. Now, before the Coal Board allowed government pay dictation to trap them in this strike, we have their word for it that they were in the black. But all that is changed. So it is significant for our case to find that in the case of the Steel Corporation, a write-off has been provided for in order to help out in a period of revenue losses.

One of the other functions of the write-off in the case of steel is to leave a reserve that can be used to deal with future closure of

* The March 1972 White Paper on 'Industrial and Regional Development' has for the first time extended Development Area capital grants to the main activities of the coal industry. This meets one of the points made by the NUM (see pages 48 and 49) but was not subsequently taken up by the Wilberforce Report (Eds.).

plants whose book value has not been fully written off. For steel, we find that the write-off is provided mainly in anticipation of the financial and accounting problems that will be caused by closures that have yet to take place. In the coal industry, although the 1965 capital write-off involved some element of anticipation, there have been over two hundred closures since then which were in no way accounted for in the write-off.

Thus, elsewhere in the British economy, over £4000 million of capital subsidy and capital write-off has been provided by the state since the last capital write-off provided for the NCB. Yet the special industrial situation of the NCB, with the problem of the long-term decline in the scale of the coal industry and the regional employment problems associated with this, obviously merit an early and major reconstruction. To repeat, since the mid-1960s the coal industry has been denied the investment grants which were extended to manufacturing, including the oil industry. It has had to borrow at fixed interest. The whole of its debt involves a fixed-interest prior charge on the accounts – although in other risky nationalized industries, notably steel and airlines, the more flexible Public Dividend Capital has been introduced. And no further reorganization of capital debt has been provided, despite a contraction of one-quarter or more in the market for coal, and the closure of nearly two hundred pits in five years.

The NUM cannot allow this vast imposition of debt and denial of adequate financial aid to the industry to operate as a denial also of adequate pay and conditions for miners. Yet the accounts to which the NCB continually refers are severely affected by this artificial continuation of a massive debt burden. The large operating surplus of the industry is concealed by massive interest and depreciation provision. This has now reached the point where the operating surplus can approach £100 million a year without the industry's accounts showing a profit. This is not a normal problem of the 'ability to pay' adequate wages by an industry. It suggests to us a much more damaging and dangerous game – one that has left the coal industry saddled with an entirely wrong financial structure, one which has held on to an increasingly deadweight debt burden. If the Treasury and the Government have thought in the past that this was one way to curb the demands of the miners, to limit them to a phoney wage fund within an artificial set of accounts, then it is time for a change.

What we are asking for is financial commonsense. And we are asking for it now. It is no use saying that we can't raise these questions because they are not in the competence of the Coal Board. We have found that collective bargaining is not in their competence either. Since it is the Government that is behind the bargaining process, since in the end it is the Government that we are bargaining with, then we say to them one of our demands is that good commonsense be applied now to the capital structure of our industry.

Since we have had to talk so much about the financial capital of the coal industry, there is one further point that the National Union of Mineworkers needs to make. The most important capital of the coal industry is quite simply the men who work in its collieries. There are about 280,000 wage earners – or were before the strike – working in the pits. At a rough estimate they had between them something like six million working years of experience in the coal industry. Of that, something near five million man-years of work have been performed underground.

On average, last year (1970–71), each of these men produced over four hundred and sixty tons of coal. This was one hundred and fifty tons more than the output per man ten years earlier. Annual production was about fourteen hundred tons for each man on the coal face – this was about six hundred tons a year more than it had been ten years earlier.

If we take the men who were working in the pits before the strike started (this is not including those who have been forced out of the industry through closures, but the lifelong output of those who still remain) we can say in round terms that these 280,000 men have between them produced about 2000 million tons of coal for the benefit of this nation. Some of these workers were there working in the pits at the time of Dunkirk (we have over 100,000 aged fifty or more, and most of those are lifelong miners). Even more were working to get the coal out at the time of the great fuel crisis in 1947. Still more of them were getting out the coal that prevented this country's economy being crippled in 1956 at the time of the Suez crisis. For many years after the war, much of the coal that they produced could have been sold at much higher prices – but instead British industry was getting its coal at a price 25 per cent less than the industries of the rest of western Europe. (So the Coal Board built up capital debt on a massive scale when it could have built up profits and revenue reserves on a massive scale.)

So, when we talk of the miners who are on strike today we are talking of men who have given some six million working years to produce some 2000 million tons of coal for the economy of this country. Without them the rest of the Coal Board's capital is worthless. Isn't it time we did our nationalized-industry accounts with the human capital of the industry properly accounted for?

Moreover, the coal industry has always been profligate in using up its human capital. The average age of a miner today is forty-four. Therefore, this 'average' miner is likely to have been working in the industry for over twenty-five years. During that time the industry has killed over 6,500 men, and inflicted over 30,000 serious injuries.*

* See also chapter 4, page 41 (Eds.).

6 The Question of Markets

Another great barrier in the way of decent treatment for mine-workers in the last decade has been the argument about the difficult market position of the industry. With this as an excuse, time and again the real rewards that we should have secured for our efforts, our skills, our productivity, have been denied us.

Before we look in detail at the market situation facing the NCB there are two comments to make. Mr Derek Ezra is something of an authority on marketing. He will agree that one factor of great significance in the long run in handling your market is that known as 'good will'. So may I emphasize the most important market with which the Coal Board is involved? It is the *labour* market – the market in which it buys men's labour power, their accumulated experience, and their very lives. And in that market the maintenance of 'good will' is supremely important, and the loss of 'good will' can cripple the effectiveness of the industry. So, in marketing, it is the job of the Coal Board to secure long-run good will in all its markets. It cannot get its approach to marketing right if it is always thinking of sacrificing good will in its labour market in the name of all the other markets that it has to consider. That good will of the miners can only be restored by recognizing the case for fair pay that the mineworkers are putting forward, and also by recognizing that the industry's management must never again abdicate its responsibility for bargaining. The future marketing strategy of the Coal Board must never forget this lesson of the strike.

There is another point. The same arguments about markets put forward to limit the offered pay concessions were also imposed on the mineworkers in an even more direct way. The miners were at the receiving end of all the insecurity, all the rough injustice of market forces when they result in closures – not just one closure which might be absorbed, but closures by the score. They were at the wrong end of the upheaval that destroyed the normal life-cycle of a miner's work, that reduced the traditional job prospects, that involved downgrading and transfers.

In 1971 hundreds of thousands of other British workers experienced precisely this phenomenon – the shock of plant closures, the scaling down of what are politely called 'labour requirements', the resultant unemployment or choice of the second-best job. They can understand what we mean. But the miners have been experiencing this since 1958 – for thirteen years. The worker who was caught in the plant closure and unemployment of 1971 must ask himself what his working life would be like if that were to continue to be his experience for another thirteen years. He would have to look forward to insecurity and upheaval from now until 1984. That year rings a bell, at least for the readers of George Orwell. That is what the miners have had to survive – not with extra rewards to compensate them but with a continued squeeze on their pay and conditions. The industry needed fewer man hours – but we are still working longer hours per shift than we did fifty years ago.

After a decade or more of living with crisis and closure, we understood that there was a change in the situation, that at long last we could discuss the needs of our men and their families against a more settled background, a brighter prospect for the industry. Thus the National Coal Board Report and Accounts 1970–71, which was published at the end of July 1971, had this to say:

Paragraph 26
The immediate and longer-term prospects of the coal industry are now brighter than they have been since 1957. During the year a severe escalation in the cost of fuel oil, which increased prices to industrial consumers by about two-thirds, gave coal a general price advantage in the industrial market. Continued technical difficulties and rapid rises in capital costs led to further delays in the expansion of nuclear power. At the same time foreign coal prices increased markedly so that the price of imported coal was generally well in excess of home-produced coal prices.

Paragraph 27
Total energy requirements continued to rise, and indications are that the conditions of world energy surplus, which existed throughout the last decade, are coming to an end. The Board consider that the country's dependence on external sources of energy should be reduced and indigenous sources promoted. In view of the technical difficulty surrounding nuclear power and the relatively modest potential contribution by natural gas and North Sea oil, the main contribution from indigenous sources to total energy requirements must come from coal.

That is clear enough, one would think. Yet, when little more than two months later we attempted to bargain with the NCB, they answered with a long catalogue of woes. Not only did they tell us that demand had been falling by a million tons a month for a year and a half, but they obviously wanted us to believe that this was some indication of the prospect for the future – since we had come to bargain about wages from November 1971 onwards.

So, how are we to view the inconsistency of the managers of an industry who speak in one way about the industry's prospects one day and quite a different way when we try to bargain with them? To cap it all, they seem to have gone back to their previous mood of optimism, if we are to judge by Mr G. C. Shephard (Board member for Industrial Relations) writing in the *Guardian* on 8 February:

We certainly do not agree that the Union sees a brighter future for coal than we in management do. . . . The coal industry, after a long period of decline, should in our view be maintained at about its present level of output.

In view of this confusion, we consider it necessary to explain why the NUM could not accept the pessimistic view of the industry's position put before them as part of the NCB's bargaining position.

The NCB made considerable play with the fact that over the last year or so the market for coal has been contracting at the rate of one million tons a month. There are a number of points that should be made:

1. This should not be linked with any alleged danger of collapse of markets due to higher prices. Inflation has been worldwide.

Other fuels have seen sharp price increases. The electricity and gas industries after major price increases at the beginning of 1971 are further increasing prices at the start of 1972 (and these increases would have been higher but for the CBI 5 per cent ceiling being imposed on nationalized industries). More important still, the increase in the wholesale price of coal over the last two years – just over 30 per cent according to the official wholesale price index – has been exactly matched by an increase of over 30 per cent in fuel oil prices. Relative coal–oil prices are virtually unchanged from two years ago – but further upward pressures on oil prices can be expected (including pressure from the oil-producing countries for an increase in royalties in dollar terms).

2. The NCB should be challenged over the alleged costs of stocking coal (due to the current imbalance between output and sales). Interest rates (especially short-term rates) are very much lower than they were last time coal stocks were built up. The NCB accounts show that there have in fact been important revenue gains made in recent years since stock when lifted has been sold at enhanced prices (as compared with price levels when stocks were laid down).

3. A number of special factors have been influencing the level of demand in the last year and a half. These either cannot be projected forward to forecast future demand trends, or will operate with diminished force. The special factors include:

the unduly slow growth of the national economy since 1969;
a major recession in steel, deepened by the running down of stocks of steel products;
the further reduction in the use of coal for conversion into gas (this process of rundown has eliminated ten million tons of coal consumption a year between 1967–8 and 1970–71, and is almost completed);
the severe reduction in the purchasing power of wage incomes and pensions during 1971 (due to price increases, a 5 per cent fall in employment in production industries; the delay until October of pension increases, etc.);
the special factor of imports contracted for in the Autumn of 1970 when coal shortages appeared imminent;

a shift to higher generating efficiency on the part of the CEGB as new stations came into operation.

So far as the forward projections of demand for coal are concerned, these must involve a marked slowing in the rate of decline experienced recently. The best estimates for the growth of the national economy suggest an annual rate of 4·5 per cent or higher, and the Government clearly anticipates sustained growth. It should be remembered that inland consumption of coal stabilized at the time of the last – unfortunately shortlived – period of rapid industrial growth in 1968 (the previous period of slow growth from 1965 to 1967 had seen a steep fall in demand). On this occasion, unlike 1968, expansion will involve a high rate of increase of consumption (and real income), which must certainly alter the trend of domestic domestic demand. There is also the special factor of the likelihood of Common Market membership; presumably the NCB would not want to suggest that exports of coal will be unaffected. (The general arguments against Common Market entry do not prevent the NUM exploring the demand forecasts of the NCB in this context.)

For all these reasons the NCB, in discussing with the NUM the market situation of the coal industry, should have looked to the future rather than concentrating on past performance. It would seem an appropriate moment to ask the NCB to make available for collective bargaining the relevant material contained in its forecasts, its Capital Development Plan, etc.

The more directly financial aspect of 'ability to pay' depends on proceeds per ton, and the intolerable burden of capital debt. What can be emphasized here are the following points:

1. The operating surplus of the NCB (before taking into account net interest payments and depreciation provision) has not moved below about £65 million a year over recent years – despite the fact that these include two periods of major decline of sales. The performance in 1970–71, with an operating surplus of about £94 million, was exceptionally strong. The operating surplus increased by over £25 million as compared with the previous year, despite a fall in sales of eleven million tons.

2. The revenue position has been further improved by the 1971 price increase. On the evidence of the wholesale price index,

this gave a further increase of about 7 per cent after the end of the 1970–71 accounting period. The average proceeds per ton in 1971–2 would appear to be over 15 per cent higher than in 1970–71. Wages (including allowances) in 1970–71 accounted for just under 40 per cent of colliery proceeds; it would be safe to estimate that wages in 1971–2 (so far) account for less than a 5 per cent increase in total costs at colliery level, as compared with 1970–71. Thus it would appear the N CB has as a residual about 10 per cent more proceeds per ton than in 1970–71 to meet any rise in unit costs other than wages and to add to its operating surplus.

3. All this is before taking into account the scope for further price increases in 1972. The 5 per cent ceiling only operates as a constraint until July 1972, and in any case has yet to be utilized. Its application in terms of marketing is helped by the price increases of gas and electricity, so that an equivalent price increase for coal would not affect what are technically known as the 'cross elasticities' of demand for coal.

What would certainly be intolerable would be to have both the artificial constraints on 'ability to pay' due to price ceilings and the continued delay in capital reorganization of the industry used as an excuse for an unjust depression of miners' pay standards. It is worth recalling that in the 1950s a similar situation arose in the railways. Understandably, the trade unions concerned would not accept a reduction in their standards and took industrial action. In the end, a careful job analysis (by a committee under Guillebaud) established that railway pay *had* fallen out of line, and by how much, and the necessary adjustment in railway pay took place. It would be a sad retreat from fair dealing if the miners in 1971–2 were to be denied even the recognition of the principle of equity extended to railwaymen in 1958.

The NUM over the years has put forward its views on a planned fuel policy that would limit our country's dependence on overseas supplies, and not waste today the natural resources under our feet that will be needed in the future too. We are not going to go in detail over that field; it would not help the Court if we did, since the Court is not in a position to judge detailed arguments as to fuel policy.

What we have to say is this:

There must be a planned and socially responsible fuel policy. It should use the rational system of social cost and benefit analysis, not be subject to the whims of day-to-day market forces and narrow commercial accounting.

After a decade and more of insecurity and suffering the miners must now ask for job security and an end to those so-called economic closures.

We want employment guarantees for the years ahead and a clear agreement that miners will not be faced with forced redundancy in the new deal that should be offered to them this week.

We are not just arguing about pay. We are arguing for an end to the insecurity that has dogged the miner's life since 1958. There is insecurity enough in our industry without that.

The inconsistencies in the NCB's attitude to the future were picked up by Laurance Hunter in an exchange with David Clement (NCB).

HUNTER: On the one hand you were saying that you were looking forward to 1972–3 with a fair degree of confidence and expectation of being able to sell about one hundred and twenty-three million tons, but on the other hand, since the increases in 1970, you have lost a substantial amount of your demand. You are now saying that there will be a market for all the coal you produce, and you do not see any reason for further closures. But some of the implications in the costing figures seem to show that costs will increase and prices will have to, unless you get productivity, and there could be more contraction of the industry.

CLEMENT: In the short term there would be a very great demand to build up the stocks of coal which had been exhausted. That changes the position slightly. Furthermore, I think the way the difficulty would be experienced – and my mining colleagues should comment on this more than I should – is that we would have a great deal of difficulty in getting our output back to the level which obtained prior to the strike. This will also have a bearing on the way the coal will go in the years ahead.

HUNTER: I will ask it another way. If the industry were rather smaller in some ways, from that point of view would it be more efficient in cost terms? Is there some special advantage, in the interest of the industry and the economy, in having this figure of an annual £135–40 million? If the contraction went on, might the price of coal per ton be brought down?

CLEMENT: As far as the total energy demand of this country is concerned, this will grow in the years ahead. There is a case for suggesting that coal, instead of being the residual beneficiary of demand, should be given a steady output to achieve. In our submission, we show estimates for demand for energy over the years ahead, and if coal were given a steady place in the energy market and the residual 'legatee' was imported oil, the country would benefit. This is the policy we would want to see.

Questioned by John Garnett, Lawrence Daly developed some of the points in this chapter.

DALY: I simply want to draw the attention of the Court to certain things arising out of this discussion about prices. The Board in its last financial year sold the product of the miner at an average price of £5.54 per ton. The other costs that a domestic or industrial consumer has to pay can in no way be attributable to the coal industry itself. This is the very low average rate at which coal is sold by the Board to the consumer. The additional costs arise from transport, by distributors, from the pithead to the consumer points and from the profit that is made, of course, by the distributor himself. I think if there is going to be any examination of the pricing policy of the Board, there is room for some examination of the other factors involved in the cost of distribution. I would also like to make the general point that in their Report published at the end of July, the Board said, on page 5 of volume 1, that 'the immediate longer-term prospects of the coal industry are now brighter than they have been since 1957'. They went on to refer to oil and nuclear power, and, at the same time, foreign coal prices –

they added – had increased markedly, 'so that the price of imported coal was generally well in excess of home-produced coal prices'.

Yet, at this moment and for some time now there have been industrial consumers importing such coal at prices well in excess, according to the Board, of home-produced coal prices and presumably still being able to use it to their commercial advantage. So, while I am not arguing the case for any general price increase in coal sold by the Board to the distributors, nevertheless it does seem to me, if some consumers are willing to pay well in excess of home-produced coal prices, the question of the price of coal should not wholly prohibit us from giving the kind of wage increase that the miners demand. . . . It is now inevitable that the industry should be provided with some assistance, whether by capital reconstruction or by other methods – by investment grants, for example.

7 What the Miners Were Offered

When the miners attempted to bargain with the NCB, essentially what happened was that they were offered the Government imposed norm or pay ceiling. For all the pay offers in the public sector this norm has been set so that it fails even to cover the rise in living costs in the last year. In real-wage terms this is familiar to those whose sense of industrial-relations history stretches back to the 1920s: 'All wages must come down.' It is an approach which pays no heed to pay problems such as have been coming to a head in the mining industry. It has sought to deny any scope for real improvement, however urgent this might be.

It is important to understand the economic consequences of a policy which seeks to curb money-wage increases while doing nothing to raise real pay and the purchasing power of incomes.

The real disposable income of workers was in total no higher in the second half of 1971 than it had been a year earlier. The impact on consumer demand acted as a curb to output. Since, at the same time, important increases in productivity were working through the economy, the result has been a steep increase in unemployment. It is clear enough that a wage offer that involves lower real disposable income than the previous settlement is a formula for increased unemployment.

The NCB in the course of the strike circulated to MPs and others examples of the effects of their rejected offer upon the disposable (post-tax) income of miners. Every single example involved a reduction in real disposable income as compared with the previous settlement. For instance, the NCB example of a power loader (with no children) showed take-home pay rising by no more than £1.29 (or 5·7 per cent), from £22.70 to £23.99, as a result of the pre-strike offer. When the rise in prices since the previous settlement is taken into account, what was on offer was a decrease in real take-home pay of about 4 per cent as compared with the settlement of November 1970.

We have illustrated, with the many examples quoted in this book, how miners' negotiated rates, gross earnings and take-home pay have failed to increase in real terms. The NCB offers are insufficient to remedy this situation. If this approach to wage settlements is to be a general one, it is a formula for lower purchasing power and deepening unemployment. Deepening unemployment was the experience of this country last year. The Government at the Treasury refused then to understand that 'de-escalation' of wages without any real-wage guarantee was a formula for creating more unemployment.

Just over a year ago Sir Douglas Allen, the head of the Treasury, giving evidence to the previous Wilberforce Inquiry, had this to say (according to the transcript for the sixth day of the hearing):

I am sure the Government will not allow a great increase of unemployment to happen. . . . *I can assure the Court* that if (and we do not agree it is likely) the situation produced a tendency for unemployment to rise, there are plenty of means the Government could take to prevent it.

That was the voice of the Treasury twelve months ago. Since then unemployment has risen by two-thirds. Four hundred thousand *more* unemployed. Five workers without a job now for every three then. Yet the Treasury did not agree a year ago that the rise in unemployment was 'likely'. They assured the previous Wilberforce Inquiry that if unemployment showed a tendency to rise there were 'plenty of means the Government could take to prevent it'. How's that for blindness?

Last year the Government's economic policy *increased* unemployment by about 60 million days. This same Government that first made the strike inevitable and then made it drag on is telling the miners that they are putting people out of jobs. We accuse *the Government* of causing mass unemployment. Their pay policies are the basic cause of unemployment today.

We now turn to the details of the latest offer that the Coal Board put to the NUM on 10 February 1972. After weeks of strike action in repudiation of the previous offer, the Coal Board produced a package that was no better than before and in a number of ways was worse than before. Neither with this nor the previous offer does the NUM consider that it is dealing with employers who had any authority to bargain seriously. The NCB offer represented an increase of about 12 per cent to last over an eighteen-month period beginning from the resumption of work.

Assuming that the agreement was envisaged as operating from the end of February, then the miners were being offered approximately 12 per cent over the eight months to the end of October 1972, instead of the previous offer of about 8 per cent for the twelve months to the end of October 1972. Either way, that means the Government's rigidly imposed pay ceiling of 8 per cent over the year – regardless of the merits of the case.

But to secure even that the miners were being asked to accept the rates of pay offered, *for a further ten months*. No protection was offered against the erosion of the purchasing power of this offer during that period; yet over the last eighteen months (July 1970 to December 1971) the retail price index rose by exactly 12 per cent.

What the offer means is this. The miners are being asked to accept a pay norm of less than 4 per cent for next year's pay round. That is all they are being offered over and above the original offer of 8 per cent. So the Government's message through the Coal Board's offer to the miners is also a message to all workers in this country: this year's pay ceiling is 8 per cent. Next year's is to be less than 4 per cent. That is what would be involved for every public-sector trade union in this country if the miners were so misguided as to accept this offer.

The offer is also offering less to the low-paid worker than might appear. It is a case of the Government knowing it will be taking back with one hand most of what the Coal Board is offering with the other hand. Thus, the low-paid surface workers are offered a £3 increase, and a £22 minimum earnings guarantee. In fact, the Government is offering them a pittance which cannot begin to compensate for the steep rise in living costs last year and in the months to come. For these low-paid workers will have to pay the full standard rate of income tax on this extra pay; they will have to pay extra national insurance too. And they are right in the middle of the income range where means-tested benefits are subject to cut-off. It can be shown that workers in this range of pay are caught in a poverty trap – a trap created by this Government's imposition simultaneously of standard income tax *and* the cut-off of means-tested benefit – so that the total effective 'marginal' tax rate becomes a very high one. What is needed if the living standards of low-paid miners are to be raised is a substantially bigger increase that will begin to pull them out of this poverty trap.*

The Coal Board proposes that the lowest rate of increase (£2.75) should apply to workers on NPLA rates. This is to ignore the fact that for years now workers in particular coalfields and many workers coming off contract work have seen their living standards falling as they sacrificed their own earnings position in the move to uniform national rates. Instead of a pay offer with a real improvement factor, the NCB are putting forward an offer with a real deterioration factor. In round terms, what the latest NCB offer means to the highest-rated men – men involved in the most arduous and skilled work in the industry – is this:

1. The man on £30 a week from the last settlement has seen his purchasing power fall by over 10 per cent since then owing to rising prices.

2. The NCB offer would start him off with real disposable income early in 1972 which would be at least 3 per cent less than at the time of the previous settlement (annual deterioration factor 3 per cent).

3. Over the first half of the eighteen months of the proposed settlement the National Institute of Economic and Social Research calculates that prices would rise 4·5 per cent in the nine months. If this is projected forward, we can say 9 per cent over the whole eighteen months. That means an annual deterioration factor of 6 per cent.

4. By the third quarter of 1973 this worker might expect to be 'enjoying' a standard of living about 12 per cent below what the NUM considers to be the inadequate level secured in November 1970.

That is the real meaning of what we have been offered so far. That is why we reject the Coal Board's offer.

* This question is developed in chapter 10, pages 92–102 (Eds.).

The economic arguments underlying this chapter were brought out as John Hughes questioned William Campbell Adamson of the CBI.

HUGHES: What would you consider to be the prospects for the profitability of industry in the coming year if there were a general reduction in the real-pay standards of workers as a result of pay settlements?

CAMPBELL ADAMSON: I want it to be perfectly clear that I am not talking about reductions in real-pay standards for workers. I want to make that clear because you have asked the question. If you ask me what would be the effect, clearly there would be some effect on profitability. Clearly there will be some upward rise in profits this year, anyway, in money terms. What I want to make clear if I can – and I think you know this very well – is that the rate of profitability over the last six years, measured in the only terms you can measure it, which is in real terms has been falling very substantially and, to my mind, dangerously.

HUGHES: May I just say I share your view on this. Can I put to you that on the most recent evidence, we appear to be operating our economy with total demand about £3000 million below what would be required for a fully employed economy?

CAMPBELL ADAMSON: I do not think I would disagree; I might argue a little bit either way.

HUGHES: Could I also put to you that there is a very direct relationship between rates of profitability and capacity utilization?

CAMPBELL ADAMSON: Certainly. Let us be clear about this one because I am very near to agreeing with you fully, but not quite. This does vary a bit from industry to industry. But I admit absolutely that in terms of the marginal units of output, the outputs not now used and brought in again, this will make a considerable difference to profitability. Indeed, if I could go further along the road to agreeing with you, it was for this reason that when the CBI took its price initiative last July, it then went to the Government and said we need this economy more related because we need this large marginal amount used. As we all know, this has been very much slower to come than we hoped; but I do not disagree with you.

HUGHES: Can I just put to you that, although we may not on this side of the table share your views on the connection between inflation and unemployment of men, there is at least a connection between unemployment of plant and inflation? I mean by that that if an industry is working with its plant heavily under-utilized, then its capital cost per unit of output are significantly higher than if we had a fully employed economy – would you disagree with that?

CAMPBELL ADAMSON: No, I would not disagree.

8 What the Miners Want

We can tell the Court in one word what it is that we want – justice.

After the years of decline in our standards – justice.

As a recognition of our enormous contribution to increased productivity – justice.

In the name of the risks we undergo, and the danger to life and limb – justice.

We are asking for £35 for our most skilled workers – those who bring most in effort, in responsibility; those whose conditions of work are most exacting and most dangerous.

We are asking for £28 as the minimum underground rate, thus creating a £2 underground work differential as against the £26 we seek for surface workers.

We emphasize that this does not restore the comparative position the mineworkers enjoyed in earnings terms some fifteen years ago. It seeks instead to recognize the rapid deterioration in the miner's relative position and in his real-wage position since about 1966–7, and to go some way to overcoming it.

If you look carefully at what we demand you will see that most of it is concerned to make up for past losses in our real standards of pay – not to establish entirely new standards. Thus the underground differential of £1 was established at that rate nearly twenty years ago. Today it is worth only half of what it was worth then – and the £2 differential that we ask for is asking, in real terms, no more than we had secured as long ago as 1953.

Earlier in our evidence we have shown two important features. One is that the pay *rates* we are talking about are the main determinant of our earnings. Other groups may conceal their earnings increases by spreading them over a bit on basic pay, some earnings drift on piecework, extra bonuses, or plus or lieu rates, and so on. Our new pay structure – which in essence is measured daywork – means the increase has to come through almost entirely on the rate itself.

Secondly, we showed that the rates of men on power loading have represented over the past five years at best a slight fall in real standards, at worst a 15 per cent or more fall.

It is because of this that we have to ask straightforwardly for an increase of £5 up to £35 for our top-rate men. £35 is a modest pay level for the most skilled men in an industry as arduous as mining. It is well below the equivalent rates in major industries such as motors.

Contrast our modest objectives with what the latest Coal Board offer involved for these men. We have shown that they were not even prepared to restore through their pay offer the real disposable income secured at the time of our November 1970 increase. And by the latter part of the period (mid-1973) during which we were to mark time, these men could expect to be more than 10 per cent worse off than in November 1970.

Nor is it unusual to have a major readjustment of pay rates after years of limited advance. It has happened recently – and with bigger increases than we are asking for – in the case of Members of Parliament. A year or so ago it happened – but on a much higher scale of increase – to such people as judges and top civil servants and to the people at the top of nationalized industries. None of them had to strike before they could get someone to listen to their special case. Nor was it immediately obvious that such people had a valid claim in terms of increased productivity such as ours.

In our demands we have continued to give priority to the lowest-paid workers. The Coal Board has given some degree of recognition of what we have been saying here by proposing larger increases for the lower-paid. Many of our lower-paid workers are older workers who have had the best part of a life of toil in the pits, and have to face much lower pay in their last years in the industry than they had earlier enjoyed. It is little enough to try to secure for them a modest level of pay. The pension from the industry that they look forward to is small enough in all conscience – £1.50 a week for what may well be fifty years of work in mining.

Besides these demands in pay rates we have also asked for the adult rate to be paid at eighteen years. The Coal Board knows, and we know, that many industries have lowered to below twenty-one for manual workers the age at which the full adult rate is secured. This has been a development of considerable importance in the last two years or so, and we consider that the coal industry should not be out of line in this respect. We have been seriously out of line in too many respects as an industry and it is time we stopped trailing behind.

In this respect, the Board knows that we expect to secure from them a third week's holiday with pay. It is obviously wrong that the coal industry, with its arduous work and so many of its workers underground, should be trailing far behind other industries – and even the ILO's convention – on holidays. And the Coal Board has already made clear to us that more holidays would not represent any significant cost to them. Instead it would positively aid more regular attendance and better health.

When our claim was originally put forward we did not think it was necessary to ask explicitly for employment guarantees, for job-security guarantees. Now we do. We want the Government to be positive and give the industry a stable future in a growth economy, to guarantee for years ahead that men can with confidence do their job secure in the knowledge that their employment security and living standards are underwritten. In that knowledge the mineworker will happily give of his best.

9 Men of Labour: The Miner's Job

And the men of labour spent their strength in daily struggling for bread to maintain the vital strength they labour with: so living in a daily circulation of sorrow, living but to work, and working but to live, as if daily bread were the only end of a wearisome life, and a wearisome life the only occasion of daily bread.

Daniel Defoe: *Robinson Crusoe*

The miner's job is dirty and dangerous. It is also one that calls for considerable manual and technical skills. The miner, too, must ungrudgingly accept a high degree of responsibility, in the efficient and careful discharge of his duties. For example, a man may shovel the same coal at a depot which was, in the first instance, shovelled by a miner at the coal face. The former is concerned almost wholly with the simple but physically strenuous process of transferring coal from one vantage point to another. He plies his manual skills with unfettered ease of movement in natural conditions. He has no control, and is not expected to exercise any control, over such conditions; and normally he is exposed to no higher degree of danger than that associated with natural conditions. The miner at the coal face must have the same manual skills as the coal-depot man – but there is no equality of comparison beyond this fact. He must shovel his coal often in very cramped conditions with pads to protect his knees as he works in a kneeling position – and his arms, also, when he is forced to lie full length on the floor. His vertical movements are restricted by the limiting interval between the roof and floor of the seam: ease of movement laterally is governed by the limiting distance between the respective lines of coal face and conveyor. He works in a poorly illuminated place with artificial light from a headpiece on his helmet. The electrical energy is provided via a cable from a battery carried on his waist belt. Also borne on his belt is a self-rescuer, an apparatus designed to give personal protection against noxious gases should he survive the initial impact of a fire and/or explosion. Additionally, he might wear a dust mask – a device with a nose-clip and mouth-filter to trap and prevent dangerous particles of dust from entering the lungs. Beside him could lie one or more canisters, which were filled with explosive cartridges at the colliery surface, and carried by him into his working place for the purpose of firing down coal from the coal face.

A flame safety lamp may be suspended from a support in close proximity. He would have charge of the lamp and use it at intervals during the working shift to test for the presence of inflammable gas as a precaution against ignitions or explosions. Air is taken to his working place as an induced current, passing firstly down one ventilating shaft before circulating the workings and being discharged upward through another shaft. On its passage through the mine the air becomes contaminated, in varying degree, by the natural heat from the strata and from machinery in operation, by inflammable gas exuding from the strata, by noxious gases produced by the use of explosives, and by rock and coal dust.

Heat and humidity in the deeper mines can have adverse physiological effects, including fatigue. Higher ventilating velocities may improve environmental conditions in this respect, but aggravate airborne dust problems by giving the air current an increased capacity to render and retain more dust airborne. The more dust that is airborne, the greater the danger of contracting pneumoconiosis and of propagating gas explosions by coal dust. High ventilating velocities provide a means for minimizing the danger of gas ignitions and explosions; and, where they must necessarily be of a high order of magnitude to dilute and render harmless inflammable gases, they cause serious discomfiture in working.

If the coal which the miner shovels has been brought down by shotfiring, he may well have bored the shotholes and assisted in stemming the shots fired – processes which, if not performed properly, may be contributory factors in an ignition or explosion of gas, or the production of relatively high concentrations of noxious gases. The miner, in shovelling away his coal, is required to support the roof newly exposed. The roof consists of beds having varying thicknesses, textures and strengths. As the coal face moves progressively forward, the roof is subject to a complex pattern of overlying pressures. The miner has a duty to safely contain such forces, wherever practicable, by the effective setting of supports – failure to do so would result in falls of roof, thereby causing accidents, increasing the danger of uncontrolled issues of inflammable gases, and impeding coal production.

In summary, the miner is seen to be a person who plies his physical and technical skills in environmental conditions which are totally unnatural. It is because of these conditions that particular problems of safety, health and production arise. It is he who has the added responsibility to help to overcome these problems. For him to be able to do so, he must possess an adequate knowledge of the principles and practice of such disciplines as ventilation, fires and explosions, gas detection, use of explosives, support and strata control, and airborne dust control. The requirement that he must be so accomplished is recognized in law – he has to satisfactorily pursue courses of statutory training before he can become a competent workman.

Mechanization and the coal-face worker

Initially, increase in coal-face production was achieved by coal-cutters travelling along the floor and face conveyors, the coal being hand-loaded on to the conveyors. Improved machines were then devised capable of simultaneously getting and loading. Many of the difficulties associated with coal-face machinery, however, were subsequently overcome by the introduction of the armoured flexible conveyor. The conveyor is so designed that it can be moved bodily sideways by mechanized means during a working shift, without the need for it to be dismantled. This innovation led to the development of coal-cutting/loading machines (power loaders) mounted on the armoured conveyors themselves, with no vertical support for the roof between the face side of the conveyor and the face line. The safe-production potential of improved coal-face machines could not possibly be realized unless they were able to operate in connection with better roof-support systems. Accordingly, wooden and rigid steel supports were replaced mainly by hydraulic props having a built-in setting device for quick operation.

Despite the improvements in supports, the increased speed of operation of the more modern power loaders exceeded the rate at which such supports could be advanced and set. To remedy the situation, the self-advancing support came into being – a hydraulically controlled unit capable not only of supporting the exposed ground after the power loader passes along the face, but also moving forward the conveyor at the same time.

The conventional coal face is now a revolutionary, complex unit of sophisticated machinery, apparatus and equipment – for cutting/loading, transportation, strata control, and for protective and communication systems. The potential of the mechanized coal face could not possibly be exploited if operators of the machinery, apparatus and equipment were not expertly trained under comprehensive training schemes of the National Coal Board, providing instruction in engineering disciplines as well as for the other skills necessary for safe and efficient coal-face work. The progress achieved can be seen from the fact that the output per manshift at the face increased from 92·9 cwt in 1963 to 143·5 cwt in 1971 – 92·2 per cent of deepmined output was won last year from mechanized faces, compared with 61·2 per cent in 1963.

The worker on the mechanized coal face has been largely spared the physical effort of the miner principally engaged in loading coal. His daily workload and his responsibilities, however, are held to be of similar weight given the greater range of technical skills he must acquire in the interests of safety, health and productivity. Indeed, he has an active concern with very expensive machinery which must normally produce a very sizeable proportion of the colliery's daily output, providing a forceful argument that his contribution is greater.

A common belief among the ill-informed is that the coal industry is technologically backward. Only a scant knowledge, however, of the tremendous reconstruction and refitting of collieries since the Second World War is needed to reverse this viewpoint.

The plant used in colliery engineering is as reliable and sophisticated as any comparable plant in any industry – and it is probably much safer.

By its very nature, coalmining has a range of safety, health and production problems uncommon in other major industries. Highest standards of engineering design, maintenance and repair, therefore, are necessary if the risks of ignitions, explosions, fires and lung disease are to be minimized and acceptable levels of production maintained at the same time.

The electrician, for example, has to cover tasks concerned with the transmission and distribution of energy and utilization of all types of equipment, such as cable jointing, switchgear, motors and control gear, intrinsically safe and flameproof gear; remote control, sequencing and interlocking circuits; signalling systems and telephone communications, etc. Similarly, the mechanic must concern himself with equipment associated with hydraulics, pneumatics, compressors, haulages, pumps, conveyors, coal preparation plants, dust control, etc.

The engineering complement at a colliery must obviously be adequate in size, technically proficient to satisfy existing requirements, and also trained to encompass the technical changes taking place.

It is a compliment to the industry's training scheme and the experience gained by apprentices in the industry that so many of them are very rapidly absorbed into other industries. For it is a fact that many of these men, having attained high technical standards, have sought or been attracted by work in other industries where conditions are more congenial and remuneration equal to, and in many cases better than, those in the coal industry.

This expensive waste of talented personnel simply cannot be tolerated if the industry is not to falter and fail.

Lawrence Daly called seven witnesses to give an account of their conditions and wages as miners.

DALY: We would like to call upon several working miners to give evidence as to their conditions and wages and I would like to call first Mr Jack Collins, who comes from a Kent coalfield.

Mr Jack Collins called

WITNESS: Mr Chairman, as Mr Daly has said, my name is Jack Collins and I am a working miner. I started work in the pits at the age of fifteen and I am now forty-two years of age. I have been in the pits for twenty-seven years. Of those twenty-seven years I have spent over twenty years at the coal face on various jobs, mainly as a ripper. Whilst not ripping I have been on other face work and have also been in headings.

In the past I have earned decent wages and I could quote an example in 1963. It was in March 1963. I can remember the date well because it was a period when I suffered a wrist injury. I have since had to go back to refer to the date in order to get a claim established with regard to the injury. At that time I was working on a ripper lip with five other men and I was receiving from the contract we were working on £5 10s. At present I am conditioned by the Third Daywage Structure and I am working at a different pit. The original pit I worked at was close to my home. I could cross the road and be there.

I am working in a pit which is much hotter than the previous one. Indeed, the men at the pit where I now work wear no clothes at all when working. This was unusual to me when I went there because I was used to working in short trousers, but eight out of ten men in the headings work with absolutely no clothes on because of the heat and, because of the amount of sweating they do, they have to drink a lot of water. Many, many men at Snow Hill Colliery drink eight pints of water a day and the Coal Board has provided them with salt tablets to put in the water to stop them getting whatever they are supposed to get by drinking a lot of water.

This is a way of encouraging the men to work in hot conditions rather than improving the conditions in the pits. What I have said is no exaggeration. It is there for everybody to see at any time. Since the advent of mechanization in the industry the amount of dust which is in the places of work has to be seen to be believed. Dust-suppression methods are used but in many cases they are not effective. I work with a dust respirator to stop the dust from going into my lungs but a number of men do not wear these masks.

I am at present working in a heading and when I am not doing that I am working at the coal face as a power loader and I am usually on a ripper lip. In 1963 I was receiving £5 10s. a shift for working at the coal face and I am now getting £5 a

shift, ten years later, and in view of that you can probably see
the feeling of the miners through me and the sort of attitude
being expressed in the picket lines, and wherever you go, as a
result of the present struggle. With regard to the new pit
where I have worked for over two years, I now have to travel
for an hour each way, whereas two or three years ago I only
had to travel across the road to go to the pit. I am away for ten
hours a day and I have to pay bus fares. It is only 25p a week,
but nevertheless this is an additional cost I have to bear.

In order to get to work on the day shift I now get out of bed
at half-past four in the morning and travel half-way across
Kent to get to the pit. I think the Court should know that I
have one child at school now and I have not been able to afford
a holiday for the last four years and I have not been away for
four years. That is fairly typical in the industry for fellows like
myself, coal-face workers, because of the wages they are
receiving. I think, Mr Chairman, that is all I can say, but I am
prepared to answer any questions.

CHAIRMAN: I would like to know, if you can tell me, how it was
that your shift payment, which was £5 10s in 1963, went down
to £5 in 1971. Was that because of the introduction of the
Third Daywage Structure?

WITNESS: Partly because of that, because in 1963 we were working on a piecework system and the piecework system gave us
an incentive to earn more money. In relation to the particular
job I am doing there were certain payments built into the contract which allowed me to receive that sort of money. Then the
power-loading method of mining came in and we negotiated
at local level a wage round about £5 a day because it was impossible, for a variety of reasons, to get the sort of money we
had been getting. Then came the National Power Loading
Agreement and later the Third Daywage Structure, which I
am now conditioned by, and I receive £5 from that. I think Mr
Daly explained that when he said that some areas were held
back and some were catching up. I was in one of the areas
which were held back.

CHAIRMAN: . . . Mr Collins, do you get any shift payments or
not, or does that not apply to your type of work?

WITNESS: No, the only shift payment I get is £5 a shift because of the example Mr Daly gave to the Court, the bonus system: if you work five shifts you get paid for six. I in fact received £30 a week.

GARNETT: You mean that you get £6 a shift now and you used to get £5.10s.?

WITNESS: I do get paid £6 a shift provided I work five shifts.

GARNETT: Am I not right that even if you work four shifts, for each of those shifts you would get £6?

WITNESS: No.

GARNETT: You only get the £6 if you work the whole of the five shifts?

WITNESS: Yes.

DALY: He would get a proportion. Four shifts at £5, if he worked four shifts, and he would get in addition one-fifth of the bonus shift added to each of these.

GARNETT: If I may say so, that makes it £6 a shift. You used to get £5 a shift and an extra £1 if you did all five.

DALY: What I am saying is this. When he was earning, in 1963, £5 10s. he had an additional 16 per cent on his weekly earnings as a piecerate worker. So it is not correct to say that he has come up to £6 from £5 10s.

WITNESS: Oh, no. When I mentioned to the Court the £5 10s a shift this was for five shifts but, of course, if I worked five shifts then, for every shift I worked I had 16 per cent of that shift in the form of a bonus, plus another 5s. make-up as well.

CHAIRMAN: I think we have got it. It is a remarkably complicated way to do what is in fact a simple sum.

HUNTER: Have you any opportunities for overtime working? Is the £30 gross pay your average or is it a little more than this?

WITNESS: Well, with regard to overtime, because I travel a long way from home and the bus into the colliery leaves my home and the colliery at a certain time – there are no bus services between shift times – there is no overtime. In fact, I do not work overtime.

HUNTER: So £30 is your pay from week to week?

WITNESS: My total pay before stoppages is about £30 and I take home a couple of coppers over £23.

CHAIRMAN: Thank you very much.

   [*The witness withdrew*]

Mr Peter Lippiat called

WITNESS: My name is Peter Lippiat, I am married, age forty-one and I work at Pye Hill Colliery in Nottinghamshire. My job at the moment is face ripper but I have been employed over the last fifteen to eighteen years on other face work and development. Up until 1967 I was always on contract work. At the end of 1967 I went on to a power-loader face at the rate of 86s. 9d. a shift, which was increased by 1s. in November 1968. At the end of 1968 I went back on to a contract face where I was earning between 110s. and 120s. a shift. Again in 1969 I went back to a power-loader face, at 92s. 1d. a shift, so a reduction of up to about £5 per week was what I suffered. I am now on a £30 a week rate. This is my position at the moment and I will answer any questions you like to put to me.

CHAIRMAN: I do not understand enough of the structure to appreciate why the contract rate was different, or how it related in terms of weekly earnings to the shift rate you had at the face, the NPLA rate.

WITNESS: The contracts were previously negotiated between the management and the workman in conjunction with the NUM.

CHAIRMAN: What is the nature of the contract job? Is it a different type of job from the one you do?

WITNESS: No, a price for a certain amount of work – for a task.

CHAIRMAN: Was it the same sort of work you were doing before on the face?

WITNESS: Oh yes.

DALY: May I explain further? When we introduced the 1966 National Power Loading Agreement it was agreed that contracts that were then in existence – for example, the producing of coal from a given section underground – would continue as locally arranged on a piece-rate system until they were worked out, and then when the man went on to another face or a team transferred to a new seam or face they would go on to the National Power Loading Agreement daywage rates. In this case, and for many other workers, that nationally agreed rate was pounds per week lower than what had been the local contract rates.

CHAIRMAN: Yes, but he seems to have got on to contract well after 1966.

DALY: He was on another job and that finished. Then if he went on to a face which was already working before he was transferred to it and was still on the locally agreed contract rate, this is exactly what could happen. He could have gone on to such a face. Then when that came to an end and he went to another one, a new face altogether, he would go on to the national daywage rates.

CHAIRMAN: The rate sticks to the face, not to the men on the face.

GARNETT: In order to compare like with like, the witness is now earning £30 a week and he was earning, under that other system, how much on a weekly basis?

WITNESS: Well, it varied between £30 and £35.

GARNETT: Was that with overtime?

WITNESS: No.

GARNETT: You quoted, I think, 120s. as a maximum.

WITNESS: No, that was not the maximum. That was approximate between 110s. and 120s.

GARNETT: That would give you for five shifts 120s. times five shifts, which would give you £30 maximum.

WITNESS: Plus 16 per cent bonus for working five shifts.

GARNETT: If you compare the job in those days with the job now, is it as grim now as it was then?

WITNESS: On the particular work that I am doing now there is no difference in the type of work whatsoever. We are still working with pick and shovel in all kinds of climates with the additional hazard of dust created by the power-loading machinery. These power loaders which are put on to the faces, and we are still working with pick and shovel in one of the gates, produce this added hazard of dust which is being created by these machines.

GARNETT: There is more than there was?

WITNESS: Yes, a great deal more.

CHAIRMAN: Thank you very much. I have got your point.

[*The witness withdrew*]

Mr James O'Connor called

WITNESS: My name is James O'Connor, I am sixty-two years of age and I have worked at Maltby since I was fifteen on all kinds of work from filling tubs in the old days and on to conveyor belts, ripping and coal heading. This coal heading is a very hard and hot job. We are ventilated by a fan and ventilation pipes and it is very, very hot. At that time, for the first seven heads that we were in I was getting an average of £6 per day plus 16 per cent bonus.

CHAIRMAN: What date are you speaking of now?

WITNESS: About 1966, just before the power loading came in. After the power loading came in, for the next two headings our particular manager would not even give us power-loading money. It was 84s. a day power-loading money, no, 83s. 10d., and he paid us 83s. 9d. He insisted on a penny differential between our wages and power-loaders' money. But we got 20 per cent on that whereas I was only getting 16 per cent on the previous wages. The last head I was in we were getting full power-loading money and 20 per cent bonus. Our wages fell down on an average; for seven heads we got £6 a day plus 16 per cent bonus. It is very hot and hard work and we were doing exactly the same work for the last three headings as we were doing for the previous one. I expected the same yardage.

CHAIRMAN: That is £6 a day, five days a week, which is £30 and 16 per cent bonus. What is that – I cannot quite do that in my head?

WITNESS: About £35.

DALY: He has lost £5 a week.

WITNESS: That was in 1966. That was when the power-loading money in South Yorkshire was only 83s. 10d. and it was 20 per cent bonus.

DALY: Has that not crept up since then?

WITNESS: It is the same as Kent and Nottinghamshire now.

DALY: But only from 1 January this year. They dropped on to much lower power-loading rates in those earlier years when these switches took place.

CHAIRMAN: Now he has got back to £30, has he?

DALY: Yes.

GARNETT: But you were on £35?

WITNESS: Yes.

DALY: It was £29 2s. 6d. prior to January.

HUNTER: Is the £30 the total gross earnings that you have from week to week or do you have something in excess because of shift allowances or overtime?

WITNESS: No, we did very little overtime. As a matter of fact I think we pushed it a bit too hard so the overtime was not necessary. We got the job done in the time required and the overtime was not necessary. We had been promised overtime if we dropped the idea of the heading. We were not getting any overtime at that time or very, very little. If anything went wrong or broke down at the weekend perhaps three men would be ordered on to do some repair work or something like that.

GARNETT: Do you get any shift addition?

WITNESS: Oh no. We were working on a four-shift system, 6 in the morning, 12 noon, 6 in the evening and 12 midnight.

GARNETT: Did you get some addition to the £30?

WITNESS: No.

DALY: The 2½p per hour which is paid extra between 8 p.m. and 6 a.m. is not paid to power-loading men. It is not paid to conventional face workers or pieceworkers or fast workers. It is merely paid to what we call the daywage men; we mean by that in the main underground transport workers and that type of worker.

GARNETT: Third-structure men?

DALY: No.

GARNETT: Black-book men?

DALY: Black-book men, that is it.

GARNETT: So far as you are concerned, Mr O'Connor, it is just £30 and nothing more?

WITNESS: So far as I am concerned it is not £30 now because I have to take a lighter job since 27 September, but up to 27 September it would be £30 if I was on national power loading now.

CHAIRMAN: Are you now on the surface or are you still underground?

WITNESS: I am underground.

CHAIRMAN: Thank you very much.

[*The witness withdrew*]

Mr David Crowther called

WITNESS: I am David Crowther and I come from Huddersfield.

I am twenty-nine and married with two children. I have been employed by the NCB at Shuttle Eye Colliery near Wakefield ever since I left school. My present position is colliery electrician, Grade 1A, away from the face, which is the highest-paid position away from the face. My gross pay is £23.40 per week, leaving me with £20.5 after standard deductions. I have been employed by the NCB at this colliery since 1958 and am now watch president at this colliery.

DALY: Would you describe to the Court what your qualifications are?

WITNESS: My technical qualifications, yes. I went to the technical college and got the ordinary national certificate in colliery electrical engineering, and then through the Mines Qualification Board I was granted my certificate of competence as a colliery electrician, Grade 1.

CHAIRMAN: How would your work compare with similar work done by people like yourself on the surface?

WITNESS: On the surface at the mine or on the surface elsewhere?

CHAIRMAN: On the surface of the mine.

WITNESS: It is a similar sort of occupation. Admittedly underground there are the hazards of the natural conditions but the actual work content, installation maintenance, is quite similar.

CHAIRMAN: How would their wages relate to yours? Would there be £1 difference or 50p or how much?

WITNESS: I believe it is between £2 and £3, the difference between the surface grade and underground.

CHAIRMAN: ... It looks as if the highest rate on the surface for similar people is £22.45 or something like that, which is about £1 less than you are getting. So £1 appears to be the difference for people working underground in your particular craft job?

WITNESS: Yes.

SHEPHARD*: Very briefly, I think the explanation is this, that Mr Crowther is employed elsewhere underground, Grade 1A, and his weekly rate for five shifts' work would equate with £23.625. Now, if he was on the surface his equivalent rate would be £21.70. You, sir, were quoting the rate at the top of

* G. Clifford Shephard is a member of the NCB.

the structure for craftsmen on the surface, for a colliery electro-mechanic, that is, a dual craft. In fact, in the industry I think we only employ eighteen of these particular people, so that is not the comparison. The comparison I have just quoted repre-sents a difference for this grade between underground and surface of £2.

GARNETT: Mr Crowther, you are, I think, listed as a craftsman here. How does this compare with a skilled electrician above ground not in mines at all but outside?

WITNESS: You have an additional responsibility. By your own actions you are responsible for the intrinsic safety of the elec-trical equipment. You are responsible for people's lives by depending upon the standard of maintenance of the equipment that you perform. This relates particularly to flame-proof equipment working in gaseous atmospheres. Relating it then away from mines to other industries as such, there are very few industries that depend on this, where your actual work has to be so critically controlled. I believe I am right in saying that the only other industry in this country where a man requires a government certificate to be able to carry on as either an electrician or a mechanic is the Merchant Navy. When you com-pare this again with other industries such as chemical engineer-ing in Huddersfield, which is maybe five miles from where I live, we had a case where a man was employed as colliery elec-trician, Grade 1, not Grade 1A, which is between £22 and £23 a week, and he moved to ICI four months ago, where as we understand it the employment situation is nowhere near as good as it has been, and he can move down there and be set on as an electrician doing similar work, but on the surface, at £31 for a basic week's wages.

GARNETT: He could be set on as a normal ETU-accepted elec-trician?

WITNESS: Yes, ETU-accepted electrician set on at £31 a week for ICI, without the hazard of working below ground.

GARNETT: To clarify this, have you yourself worked a five-year apprenticeship or something like that?

WITNESS: Yes, I served my apprenticeship and was in college up to ordinary-certificate level.

DALY: The qualifications of electricians are indeed very high because it is accepted that the Coal Board's training scheme for craftsmen is probably the very best in the country. I would like to ask you, Mr Crowther, if you have much opportunity to get extra earnings through overtime.

WITNESS: As a craftsman I have these opportunities. There is no doubt about it, I can improve my earnings with overtime. As to the reason why this is brought about, it is due to the shortage in the number of craftsmen. As to why we are short of craftsmen, maybe my illustration about the I CI explains this without going any further into it.

GARNETT: Can you tell us how many hours' overtime you are actually working?

WITNESS: At the moment I am not working!

GARNETT: When you were last working overtime, how much overtime were you working?

WITNESS: At that time I think we averaged amongst the whole workshop approximately one hour per day during the week, a Saturday morning which is another five hours, and possibly occasionally a Sunday morning, which is a second five hours.

GARNETT: Making fifteen hours a week?

WITNESS: This was fifteen hours a week, yes. That is on top of the basic thirty-six-and-a-quarter-hour week.

CHAIRMAN: That, I think, is fairly exceptional, is it not?

WITNESS: I think you will find within the industry that it is nothing near exceptional for craftsmen as such.

CHAIRMAN: But apart from craftsmen it is exceptional?

WITNESS: Yes, apart from craftsmen it is exceptional.

DALY: In view of the fact that apparently unless you work this type of overtime much of the maintenance and repair work underground could not be done, could you say if in your opinion the shortage of craftsmen because of these low wages has any influence in holding down the production level at your own pit?

WITNESS: At my own pit I should say that it has. You see, my colliery is not mechanized as such, if we have been talking in terms of mechanization this afternoon. At collieries where we have mechanization and a much larger quantity of complex machinery, the fact that there is a shortage of craftsmen must affect the maintenance to some extent and consequently must affect the profitability of the machinery and the production level as such.

HUNTER: When you say that there is a shortage of craftsmen, are there actually jobs vacant at the pit?

WITNESS: There are vacancies.

HUNTER: How many craftsmen would you expect normally to be employed?

WITNESS: I am talking about a very small colliery but I should say that we could find work at our colliery for 33 per cent more craftsmen.

GARNETT: With this very heavy overtime, what do your earnings come out at?

WITNESS: It is possible to earn £30 a week but I have to work ten hours overtime at time-and-a-half rate. That is gross earnings. Consequently, when I do work on a Sunday at double rate I may have gross earnings, of approximately £35 a week.

CHAIRMAN: Thank you very much.

[*The witness withdrew*]

Mr Jesse Tonge called

WITNESS: My name is Jesse Tonge, aged fifty-one, married with two children grown up and working. Colliery – Agecroft, near Manchester. Job – surface worker Grade 2, fork-lift truck driver. My evidence is – no chance of overtime, so I am on the minimum rate. After deductions for tax and national Insurance, Union dues, pension scheme, my take-home pay is £15 per week. I have not worked overtime for the past two years. I have some photostat copies of my pay slips here.

CHAIRMAN: I am not sure that I have got all that. Fifteen pounds is your take-home pay. What is your gross pay?

WITNESS: £18.

CHAIRMAN: How long have you been on that? When did your last increase happen?

WITNESS: November 1970.

DALY: Do you have any opportunities to work overtime?

WITNESS: None whatsoever.

GARNETT: For how long have you been a fork-lift-truck driver at the colliery?

WITNESS: Since 1961.

DALY: Have you ever worked underground?

WITNESS: Yes, up to 1950.

DALY: Can you explain why you came up to work on the surface?

WITNESS: I came up with chest trouble, and I could not go down again.

DALY: What would be the reduction in your earnings when you were forced, because of your chest condition, to come from underground up to the surface job, roughly?

WITNESS: Oh, I was a face worker at the time.

DALY: You were a face worker up to 1950?

WITNESS: Yes.

DALY: I appreciate that it is a long time to remember back, but there would be, I think, at that time as well as today, a very substantial reduction in your earnings because of your chest condition?

CHAIRMAN: We can assume that there would be a reduction, yes.

GARNETT: As a 'truck driver' – that means as a lorry driver, does it?

WITNESS: No, a fork-lift-truck driver.

DALY: Do you live in a council house?

WITNESS: Yes.

DALY: He has a take-home pay of £15 per week. Of that £15, what do you pay for rent?

WITNESS: Just over £3 per week.

DALY: And, although you are a fork-lift-truck driver, you have no differential for that skill at all; you are on the minimum rate in the mining industry?

WITNESS: On the minimum, Grade 2.

HUNTER: How does that £18 compare with what might be obtained by a fork-lift-truck driver in factories nearby in your area?

WITNESS: The difference?

HUNTER: Yes, in terms of basic rates?

WITNESS: Well, it is different in different firms, is it not? I would get, I should think, about £30 per week.

GARNETT: Why don't you leave and get that job?

WITNESS: Because I have so much to lose if I leave the colliery.

GARNETT: What would you lose?

WITNESS: Well, my pension and so on.

GARNETT: Could you go on a bit about the 'and so on'?

WITNESS: Well, there is my pension, concessionary coal, there are more holidays – with rest-days that is; I get more pay for rest-days than I do when I am working, which is true.

GARNETT: Could you just explain that to me?

WITNESS: When we are on holiday, the surface workers and the daywage workers, we earn more money for holidays than what we have when we are working.

GARNETT: Can anybody explain how that comes about?

WITNESS: Because the agreement between the National Coal Board and the Union was that they would come to a final figure, and we get paid the same as the underground face worker for holidays.

DALY: The holiday daily payment is based on a calculation taking the annual gross earnings in fifty weeks of the year and dividing it by the number of manshifts, and the consequence is that average figure, whatever it is, is paid to every man in the industry, so that the lower-paid people actually get an increase when they are on holiday and the higher-paid get a reduction.

GARNETT: That is a tradition going back a long time, is it?

DALY: I am sorry – a slight correction: as I said, it is fifty weeks – a year's gross earnings are divided by fifty; that gives you the weekly rate for a week's holiday, and then gives you the daily rate. Everybody gets paid that average, so again, I repeat, the lower-paid man gets an increase when he is on holiday and the higher-paid man gets a reduction.

GARNETT: And how long has it been like that – or has it always been the case?

WITNESS: Well, for twenty years anyway – since 1946, I would say.

CHAIRMAN: May I ask you how good your state of health is at the present time?

WITNESS: Well, it is not what it should be, by far; but I have been worse.

CHAIRMAN: You could not go back and work underground, for example?

WITNESS: Oh no, the doctor would not let me go.

CHAIRMAN: Could you go and do a job similar to that which you are holding at the moment in an outside firm?

WITNESS: On the shop floor, yes.

DALY: But with such jobs, though, in factories, etc., of a similar nature to yours, where you have indicated that there are higher wages, would it be easy to obtain such a job? Are there many of these jobs going?

WITNESS: No. It would be a little difficult at my age at any rate. They are asking for them, but it is the security at the back of the job when you get it.

CHAIRMAN: Thank you.

[*The witness withdrew*]

Mr Alan Carter called

WITNESS: My name is Alan Carter, I am thirty-three years old; I am married with four children. I work at Mardy Colliery in the Rhondda Valley in South Wales. I am a surface Grade 2 worker doing jobs which include driving a diesel loco, a Coles crane, and a sixteen-cubic-yard Euclid lorry. I have a basic wage of £18 per week, and my take-home pay is less than £17 for a wife and four children. My earnings are so low that I qualify for family supplement which include free milk, school milk for my children, and welfare foods for the baby. The chances for doing overtime are very scarce, unless I am driving the Euclid lorry, when I get a Saturday morning maintenance; other than that, it is only covering absenteeism.

DALY: Can you tell us what the value of the means-tested benefits you are getting comes to?

WITNESS: My free milk amounts to £1.15 a week; the school meals, £1.20 per week, and I have got a family supplementary pension book on which I get £1.70 a week; this will be increased on 1 April to £2.70; at the present time it is over £4 in benefits, but on 1 April it will be over £5 – unless we have a substantial pay offer.

CHAIRMAN: Your Grade 2 includes people doing any job on the surface; is that right?

WITNESS: Any job. The only difference, I should point out, is that when we are driving a Euclid lorry, owing to this lorry being of over 250 horse-power, I get an extra rate of about 2½p per day.

CHAIRMAN: Are you able to compare your pay with that of people driving similar things round about, in local government or something of that sort?

WITNESS: There are people working at Baglan Bay with exactly the same lorries earning anything from £30 to £35 per week.

CHAIRMAN: I am not quite sure what a Euclid lorry is.

WITNESS: It is a big American lorry for conveying pit muck from the pit; and the people at Baglan Bay driving these lorries do not have it half as bad as what we are having it.

GARNETT: Why don't you leave the Coal Board, then?

WITNESS: It is a matter of getting out to this place: it is the best part of fifty miles away there and back, and there is no way of getting there unless you have your own car.

GARNETT: And there is no equivalent work nearby?

WITNESS: No.

CHAIRMAN: You have been born and brought up, have you, in the Rhondda?

WITNESS: No. I have lived in the Rhondda for ten years.

CHAIRMAN: Always in the same job, or did you start in another job?

WITNESS: I have been in the coal industry for ten years.

HUNTER: Are you unable to move to work underground, where you might get higher earnings?

WITNESS: Well, I have always worked on the surface; I have never worked underground. I have never done underground training.

HUNTER: This is a decision on your part, rather than a shortage of opportunities to go underground?

WITNESS: On my part to work on the surface, yes.

HUNTER: Are there any promotions that you can look for or expect, or any increases or improvements?

WITNESS: The only promotion I can get on the surface is from loading timber to driving a lorry, which is about 45p per week. It puts my money up from a basic of £18 to £18.45.

HUNTER: This would be a transfer *to* driving?

WITNESS: Yes. I am classed as a 'spare-hand' driver on top of the pit.

HUNTER: Did you also say something about driving a diesel?

WITNESS: Yes, a small diesel loco, which is used for shunting supplies around at the top of the pit, and a Coles crane.

HUNTER: So you are very versatile?

WITNESS: Yes.

GARNETT: When you are on the loco, are you on a higher rate?

WITNESS: No, we are still on the same rate; we lost the differential for the loco with the last pay award.

CHAIRMAN: Thank you very much.

[*The witness withdrew*]

Mr Gerald Thorne called

WITNESS: My name is Gerald Thorne. I come from Pontypridd. I work at Coedely Colliery. My age is thirty-three, I am married with five children. My job is a rope changer underground, Grade 3. My basic wage is £19 per week. After deductions, I give my wife £17 a week. My earnings are so low that I qualify for the whole range of government means-tested benefits on the income supplement: free school meals, free milk, welfare foods, prescription charges, health charges. I have got books to produce and dockets of my last pay packet. My overtime is very little, only through absenteeism.

DALY: Again, what is the value of the means-tested benefits?

WITNESS: I get £1.40 from the family supplements; I get free milk which is valued at 38½ pence, i.e. one pint per day; I get free school meals, which is £2.40, which comes to a total of £4.18½ pence. I also get free prescriptions, on which I have had five items since I have had this, which comes to £1; I also have two grants for my children to go to school, valued at £10 for uniforms.

DALY: And you have to go through a means test in order to qualify?

WITNESS: Yes.

CHAIRMAN: Is your gross pay £19 or a bit more?

WITNESS: £19 is my gross wage.

GARNETT: I could not catch what you said about overtime and absenteeism?

WITNESS: There is very little overtime unless there is somebody missing – absenteeism.

GARNETT: And in practice, going back a bit – I mean, when things were normal – was there much overtime?

WITNESS: No, there has never been much overtime in this job.

GARNETT: Because there is not much absenteeism?

WITNESS: Because there is not much absenteeism on the job I am on, no.

GARNETT: Is this skilled work of splicing wires and things of that sort?

WITNESS: No, no; this is rope changing. That means that I convey materials from the pit bottom where we work into the 'inside paddy', as we call it; it is a journey of timber.

DALY: What is the position in regard to your rent?

WITNESS: Well, I pay £3.73 rent, and I have got to pay that out of my wages.

HUNTER: For how long have you been doing this job?

WITNESS: I have been on this low-paid job since January 1970.

HUNTER: Did you do another job before that?

WITNESS: I was on the coal face before that, and I had to come up through illness and accidents.

HUNTER: Do you have any other opportunities, apart from going back to the face, to increase your earnings?

WITNESS: No. This is the only job I can do now.

CHAIRMAN: Thank you, Mr Thorne, for your evidence.

[*The witness withdrew*]

10 The Malaise of the Low-Paid Worker

Evidence of Michael Meacher

Undoubtedly one of the general causes underlying the present dispute is the deep sense of frustration felt by hundreds of thousands of workers that they are increasingly caught in a poverty trap. The trap is produced by a conjunction of factors which collectively are diminishing the capacity of the low-paid to improve their standard of living almost to vanishing point.

These factors comprise the increasing bite of income tax among the low-paid, growing inflation which hits the lowest-paid hardest, and the accumulation of means-tested benefits which were designed as a remedy to this dilemma but which have in fact generated a sharp disincentive effect. All these factors have operated against a background of an anyway relatively declining position of the lower-paid over this last decade.

The drop in the tax threshold

The most profound restriction on the growth of real disposable income (real take-home pay) over this last decade has undoubtedly been the increasing bite of income tax. Table 8 makes it clear that the enormous expansion in the scope of income tax since the Second World War, which has accelerated particularly in the last decade, has been chiefly at the expense of the lower-paid because of the sharp drop of the tax threshold. For a married man with two children the tax threshold hovered around national average earnings levels for ten years after the Second World War, since when it has steadily fallen till it is now little over half that level.

The faster rate of inflation has thus not only eroded the purchasing power of real disposable income, but has catapulted money incomes into the tax brackets for the first time for millions of lower-paid workers. This process has been exacerbated by the recent introduction of the clawback device and the abolition of

Table 8 **Impact of income tax on the lower paid, 1938–1971**

Date	Tax threshold for a married man with two children as proportion of national average earnings %
1938–9	209·5
1946–7	102·9
1959–60	82·2
1964–5	78·1
1967–8	66·0
1971–2	58·6

Source: *Hansard*, 4 February 1972 and 14 February 1972

the reduced rate bands for income tax. Nor has this been compensated by a corresponding increase in tax allowances.

The net effect on the low-paid worker is revealed by Table 9, which shows that income tax now becomes payable *below* the level at which supplementary-benefit entitlement begins in the case of single persons and childless couples, and only marginally above this point where there are children. Indeed, income tax in Britain has a harsher impact on those below £2000 a year, and above all on those around £1000 a year, than in any other comparable major advanced industrial country.

Table 9 **The relation between supplementary-benefit levels and the tax threshold, 1971–1972**

Household type	Earnings necessary to reach supplementary benefit level £	Earnings threshold for income tax £
Single person	12.40	8.05
Married couple without children	16.40	11.50
Married couple with 2 children under 11	17.04	17.25
Married couple with 4 children under 11	20.24	20.85

Table 10 **Gross money income, deductions and net income of a median wage-earner, married with two children**

Year	Gross earnings plus family allowance £	Income tax (PAYE) £	National insurance contributions £	Net money incomes £	Net real income (at 1959 prices) £	Income tax and National insurance contributions as percentage of gross earnings, plus family allowances
1959	687	12	26	648	648	6
1962	801	31	41	729	669	9
1966	1030	59	56	915	732	12
1969	1269	146	67	1056	748	17
1970	1420	186	83	1151	768	19

Source: H. A. Turner and F. Wilkinson, 'Real net incomes and the wage explosion', *New Society*, 25 February 1971. The final column has been added to the original.

The impact of tax on low incomes

These processes have meant that the proportion of the average-paid manual worker's gross income taken by income tax and social insurance contributions has risen from slightly 'over 5 per cent in 1959 to nearly 20 per cent in 1970'.* In other words, the proportion of gross earnings taken by direct taxes has more than trebled in this period. The combination of this effect with inflation is traced in Table 10. It demonstrates that though gross earnings plus family allowances more than doubled over the last decade, net real income for the average wage-earner rose only 19 per cent. It is probable that 'any group of wage-earners whose rate of pay rise between 1965 and 1969 lagged much more than 1 per cent behind the annual national average increase in earnings probably suffered an actual *fall* in real living standards'.

Means-tested benefits: either low take-up or disincentive

Besides the worsening relative position of the low-paid and the mutually reinforcing factors of price erosion and a sharply rising tax-take, a third factor which has unwittingly contributed to the poverty trap for the low-paid is the Government's policy of resorting to means-tested benefits as the main technique for supplementing low wages outside the market. The main benefits involved here are the family income supplement (FIS), free school meals, school uniform/clothing grants, education maintenance allowances, rent rebates, rate rebates, free welfare foods, and exemption from prescription, dental and optical charges.

To the extent that these benefits are actually claimed by low-paid workers, they may well in some cases provide a significant extra source of income. Such information as is known about the level of take-up and the weekly value of each of these benefits is given in Table 11 (pages 96–7). This Table illustrates the following points:

1. The cut-off point for eligibility for these benefits lies within the £18–£24 per week income band and is centred chiefly around the £21–£24 per week mark.

* The quotation and substance of the paragraph are taken from H. A. Turner and F. Wilkinson, 'Real net incomes and the wage explosion', *New Society*, 25 February 1971.

Table 11 The main means-tested benefits available to low-income workers, their value and their degree of take-up

Means-tested benefit	Estimated number in regular receipt annually	Estimated total number of eligible recipients	Annual Exchequer cost (£m)	Average weekly value of benefit*	Income limit for eligibility*	Take-up data source
FIS	120,000 (75%)?	165,000	7	£1.72	£21.80	Hansard, 9 Dec. 1971
Free school meals	805,000 (over 80%)?	1,000,000?	28?	87½p	£22.80	Hansard, 3 Dec. 1971
School uniform/clothing grants	400,000 (40%)?	1,000,000?	nk	nk	£22.80 approx.	New Society, 24 Nov. 1966
Educational maintenance allowances	20,082 (20%)?	100,000?	0·75?	50p–£1	nk	DHSS questionnaire, 1970
Rent rebates†	425,000	nk	18·5	87p	£16 approx.	Housing Statistics, IMTA, 1970
Rate rebates	795,302 (25%)?	3,000,000	14·6	35p	£18.25	Rate rebates in England and Wales, 1971
Free welfare foods	200,000‡	nk	7·5**	75p	£23.60	Hansard, 9 Dec. 1971

Exemption from prescription charges	990,000§	nk	nk	nk	£22.35	Hansard, 9 Dec. 1971
Exemption from dental charges	100,000‡	nk	2**	6p	£23.80	Hansard, 9 Dec. 1971
Exemption from optical charges	150,000‡	nk	3·5**	7p	£23.80	Hansard, 9 Dec. 1971

nk = not known

* For a man, married (wife not working) with 3 children (aged 4, 7 and 11) and rent £3 per week; it also includes family allowances.

† Take-up will be expanded to a potential eligible total of some 3½–4 million families if the Housing Finance Bill becomes law.

‡ Includes those in receipt of these benefits on grounds of low income, but not in receipt of supplementary benefit.

** Includes payments for charges incurred by persons in receipt of weekly supplementary benefit and FIS as well as by persons not in receipt of either of these benefits.

§ Includes those exempt from prescription charges on grounds of receipt of supplementary benefits or FIS as well as on grounds of low income.

2. The average value of benefits varies greatly, from relatively minor amounts to £1.72 per week in the case of FIS, and 87·5p per week per child for free school meals.

3. Eligibility totals, with the one exception of FIS, are not known with any certainty, so that estimates of take-up levels are very approximate. But in general they vary from 20 per cent or lower in the case of educational maintenance allowances to 80 per cent or more in the case of free school meals.

4. Families in regular receipt of these benefits vary widely between totals of 100,000 and 400,000 (embracing some 800,000 free-school-meals children).

The dilemma in which means-tested benefits place low-paid workers is this. Either these benefits are not claimed, in which case *ipso facto* they fail to resolve the problem of low wages; or they *are* claimed, in which case the problem of disincentive arises. The latter comprises the high marginal 'tax' levy in terms of benefit foregone as well as further tax payable on increased earnings within the bands for different benefits, which closely overlap in the £16–£28 weekly income range, between maximum entitlement to these benefits and their cut-off points. Both of these arms of the dilemma will now be examined further.

It may be that, whether for reasons of ignorance, fear of stigma, fear of upsetting the landlord/employer, etc., low-paid families do not take up their means-tested entitlements. Whilst this certainly remains partly true, the Government has successfully sought, through extensive advertising and other promotional campaigns, to raise take-up appreciably, at least in the case of a range of benefits associated with FIS. The exemptions from the various NHS charges have been increased by three-and-a-half to four-and-a-half times since April 1971 and the take-up of free welfare foods has actually been increased some sixty times. Furthermore, the take-up of FIS in the higher ranges of award has been quickly raised to the point where about 63 per cent of those entitled to £1–£1.90 and about 83 per cent of those entitled to £2–£4 under this benefit are now receiving it (*Hansard*, 19 January 1972). It can therefore be reasonably assumed that:

1. Of those eligible for the more valuable benefits, FIS and free school meals (i.e. those in the income band £18–25 per week –

and 64 per cent of miners at present grade rates are within this band) between three-fifths and four-fifths are receiving these entitlements.

2. Take-up of other educational welfare benefits remains low.

3. Take-up of housing-welfare benefits, rent rebates and rate rebates, remains extremely low or almost non-existent for low-paid workers because the ceiling for eligibility in their case is almost always too low. To that extent these charges remain at present a regressive tax that particularly penalizes the lower-paid.

On the other hand, to the extent that most of the lower-paid workers now eligible for the most valuable benefits do receive them, the remaining component of the poverty trap now confronts them. This is that for each extra £1 of earnings obtained over the range from the very low pay to above-average pay, large deductions will be made arising from income tax (30p in £), national insurance and superannuation payments (10p in £), FIS (50p in £), school meals (60p in £), and rent and rate rebates (8½–17p in £), all mutually reinforcing each other in their effects in an arbitrarily varying manner throughout the income range in question. Table 12 (page 100) traces these effects at the present time.

It must of course be remembered that these are net gains from increased earnings *before* the reduction of purchasing power from rising prices is calculated, and it is clear that in almost every case in the £18–£25 income range at issue inflation would have far more than wiped out any net gain altogether, compounding in some cases what were *already* substantial losses.

But even *before* price erosion is taken into account, Table 12 illustrates that the amounts left over after tax and benefits foregone are in most cases negligible and certainly arranged in an arbitrary formation that makes a mockery of calculated incentives. It is clear also that this deterrent effect is paradoxically exacerbated by the Government's success in promoting higher take-up of a range of means-tested family welfare benefits, because more workers are affected by the consequential disincentive to increase earnings except in large amounts, and for workers already claiming some means-tested benefits the disincentive is reinforced.

Table 12 Amount remaining from £1 increase in earnings at different income levels*

Weekly earnings £	Amount remaining to family with 2 children (aged 6 and 8) pence per £ increase	Amount remaining to family with 3 children (aged 7, 9 and 11) pence per £ increase
14–15	33½	30
15–16	35½	35½
16–17	26½	35½
17–18	20	32½
18–19	1	22½
19–20	−10	19
20–21	−10	8
21–22	5	−9
22–23	35½	5
23–24	44	22
24–25	45	45
25–26	44	45
26–27	44	43
27–28	45	45
28–29	−42	44
29–30	nil	−41
30–31	5	nil
31–32	43	4
32–33	45	−1
33–34	45	45
34–35	43	44

Summary

There is clear evidence that the combined interaction of three factors is producing a poverty trap for the lower-paid from which they cannot escape without disproportionately large wage-increases. These factors are:

1. The sharp drop in the tax threshold leading to an enormously disproportionate increase in the tax-take relative to gross wages,

* The 1972 Budget has raised the tax threshold (as compared with the figures in Table 9); however, it has left virtually unchanged the high effective tax rates above the threshold (shown in Table 12) (Eds.).

especially for the lower-paid in recent years.

2. The considerable extension of the coverage of means-tested benefits which, if rejected, loses the only non-market assistance available to supplement low wages, and which, if accepted, very markedly diminishes the capacity to make any further real gains in the market.

3. The acceleration of price inflation leading to a large upward float of money wages without more than a marginal increase in purchasing power.

It is the *conjunction* of these factors rather than any one in isolation which constitutes the poverty trap and which, even if not fully understood, is increasingly leading to an accurate awareness that only very substantial increases in low wages, that take workers beyond the area where these factors concur, offer a way out.

Lord Wilberforce summed up the argument of this chapter.

CHAIRMAN: Thank you very much. It is a very interesting paper. Of course, you know much better than we do that many of the matters raised here are quite beyond our competence. It is really the moral you wish us to draw in this, i.e. that the combination of these factors does explain the fact that wage demands do tend to be at first sight very large. . . . The gist of what you wish us to draw is that that applies, on your statistics (which we want to look into carefully), with special force to the coalmining industry. . . . I am rightly summarizing the lesson you want us to draw from the paper?

MEACHER: That is right. I think it is only large increases which can give any net gain at all. Although one appreciates the consequences of this in other ways, in terms of actually improving living standards for the lower-paid, there is no other way out. One has to get the lower-paid as rapidly as possible beyond this concurrence of factors. This does apply particularly to the coal industry, which I take to be a particular instance of the general case which I am making. The evidence has already indicated that the combination of tax and prices can, in some cases that have been quoted in chapter 2 of the evidence, on pages 28 and

29, actually lead to reduced real pay. What I have done is to show (which I think is omitted from that evidence) the further effects of the conjunction of means-tested benefits at this point and to calculate quantitatively some of those effects.

HUNTER: I wonder whether this is the right lesson that one should take from this. Surely one alternative would be to get rid of the concurrence of circumstances or effects? This surely must be the answer rather than trying to get round it by individual wage increases which try to get over this particular barrier at the same time as the barrier itself may be shifting.

MEACHER: I think both are necessary. I think it is certainly the case that one ought to aim to raise the tax threshold. Whether or not one likes the use of means-tested benefits to supplement low wages is a matter for some controversy; but it does exacerbate it. It would make it easier if one reduced the means-tested ones; it would be easier to achieve the kind of results one wants if prices did not rise so fast. But even so, the capacity to do this economically, raise the tax threshold £5 or £10, which is the order of magnitude required, would cost again in the order of £8–12,000 million in lost revenue. It is very easy to suppose one can do it in other ways. Certainly employers or the unions cannot do it alone. The Government must take a hand; but I do not think it can do it alone either. I do not think one can ignore the central importance of wage increases for the low-paid in this matter.

HUNTER: One can go through the situation of the low-paid receiving large increases but what worries me is that one has not solved the problem at all. It seems to me one wants to get away from a very distinct policy in this and not necessarily by trying to tackle it through individual wage increases.

MEACHER: I would agree with that. It must be, as I say, a joint programme. But I do not think one can raise the tax threshold overnight by that much; nor, unless there is some attempt to prop up low wages by other means, do I think that one can fade down means-tested benefits. So one is still left with the problem which I think does lie with employers and unions; and it can only be so far assisted by the Government.

CHAIRMAN: . . . There is a lot of food for thought in your interesting paper. We will give it careful consideration.

Lord Wilberforce identified a further interesting economic implication of the kind of analysis presented in this chapter in his questioning of William Campbell Adamson (CBI).

CHAIRMAN: You point out that there are people who suffer very much from inflation and say that the CBI has their situation very much in mind. There is, of course, this point: that if increases concentrated largely on the lower-paid workers that would help to increase demand, which is I think a problem you are anxious about, and therefore to that extent it is in the right direction of possibly reducing unemployment. I just put this to you because your paper [not included here] does not deal with the demand or consumer aspect, which I should have thought was a necessary other side to the question of settlements.

CAMPBELL ADAMSON: The paper is very short, partly, I think you will appreciate, out of consideration for the time at your disposal. Certainly the increases to lower-paid workers will affect consumer demand. We are more concerned in this case, of course, with the effects of increases or negotiations in settlements following this settlement, which might take into account not only lower-paid workers but workers as a whole. It is a moot point at the moment whether we want demand further increased or not. It may well be the case that we require demand further increased. But it is the way in which one increases demand that makes so much difference to what happens afterwards.

CHAIRMAN: I only mention this because there are quite a number of lower-paid workers in the coalmining industry, and that is part of the problem. I do not gather there is any great disagreement between you and those who are concerned with the case of the lower-paid workers in the coalmining industry.

CAMPBELL ADAMSON: None at all. In fact we have noted in our document here that, with satisfaction, we saw the last offer, which to our minds did do quite a lot for low-paid workers.

11 Exceptional Pay Settlements

Evidence of Hugh Clegg

I want to argue that our industrial-relations system is in need of some permanent provision whereby consideration can be given to the case for exceptional pay increases in industries and undertakings in a situation such as that of the coalmining industry over the last year or so. There are seven steps in the argument.

The first is the well-known tendency, under inflation, for earnings to rise faster where pay is settled domestically in each plant (especially under systems of payment by results) than where pay is settled in central industry-wide negotiations (especially where time rates are the rule).

The second step is the increasingly clear-cut division in postwar Britain between public industries and services whose pay is settled centrally, in most instances on a timework basis, and private industries where domestic bargaining is widespread.

The third step is the obligation which governments have come to accept more and more readily to exercise (whether overtly or covertly) some control over the general level of pay, and therefore especially over the pay of those industries and services where they have some degree of authority, such as the public services and the nationalized industries. Government policy has therefore reinforced the tendency of public-sector pay to fall behind.

These three features of our industrial-relations system have brought a series of conflicts between governments and groups of public employees. Railway pay dropped behind the general level during the 1948–50 period of wage restraint, and there was a run of strike threats and one major strike over the next decade until the Guillebaud Committee was appointed in 1958. London busmen had been falling behind over a considerably longer period when they came out in the prolonged strike of 1958, which ultimately led to the appointment of the Phelps-Brown Committee. The 'status' agreements in electricity supply brought higher hourly earnings but a relative decline in weekly earnings, which provided the background to the work-to-rule in 1969 and the last Wilberforce Inquiry.

However, if all this is established, it seems reasonable to ask why there is not continual ferment throughout the public sector. The answer lies in the fourth and fifth steps of my argument. The fourth is that trouble has concentrated, as might be expected, where there are powerful unions. The Railwaymen and Locomotive Engineers, the London busmen's section of the Transport and General Workers, andt he several unions in electricity supply are more likely to be provoked into industrial action than, say, health-service and local-authority employees – although the 'dustmen's' strike shows that trouble can arise in those quarters.

The fifth step is the protection that has been given to some public employees to insulate them from the effects of the process I have described. Since the Priestley Report in 1955, non-industrial civil servants have enjoyed the benefits of an elaborate system of pay comparisons intended to ensure that they can earn as much as their 'outside analogues'. In times of stress governments have delayed the operation of this system for a time, but they have not dared to abrogate it. And more recently, outside earnings over the standard week have replaced basic rates as the proper basis for settling the pay of industrial civil servants.

This point leads directly to my sixth step, which is that favourable consideration of claims for exceptional treatment has led to lasting improvements in pay. The application of the Priestley Report raised the relative pay of non-industrial civil servants, which had fallen behind during the war, and sustained the new relationship. The Guillebaud Report led to a similar change in the relative pay of railwaymen, as did the Phelps-Brown Report in the relative pay of London busmen. It is too soon yet to judge the effect of last year's report on the pay of electricity-supply workers, but it is at least clear that during 1971 their earnings rose considerably faster than the level of earnings elsewhere.

It is sometimes said that it would be self-defeating to raise the miners' pay by x per cent above the original offer because subsequent settlements elsewhere would then be x per cent higher than otherwise, until at the end of twelve months the original relationships would be restored, and prices would meanwhile also have risen by x per cent or thereabouts. However, the evidence of past instances of special treatment for exceptional cases points in the other direction. It has proved possible to achieve lasting remedies for maladjustments in pay.

The seventh and final step is to show that the miners' position is similar to that of the groups I have quoted, and the similarities are evident. The miners work for a nationalized industry. Since the 1966 Power Loading Agreement transferred face workers to timework, the great majority of coalminers have been on time rates. They have a powerful trade union. Detailed comparisons of the pay movements of miners and other workers are outlined elsewhere; they show that the miners have slipped back since the Power Loading Agreement. I do not need to repeat them, nor have I the material available for a full analysis.

I should, however, like to add one further point which emphasizes the miners' claim for special treatment. One consequence of the Power Loading Agreement was to hold back the pay of most face workers in relation to the rest of the industry, and to hold back the pay of some groups of face workers far more than others. It is, I believe, generally agreed by practitioners of industrial relations that, when a new pay structure alters the relative pay of groups of workers in an industry or undertaking, there is need for a generous overall increase to be injected, so that all, or all but a few, of the workers who suffer a relative setback should, nevertheless, receive a net advance. But over the last few years a large number of miners have been asked to take a reduction relative to the general level of miners' earnings at a time when that general level has been falling behind the movement of pay in the country as a whole.

This is not to say that there should be no relative changes in pay. A dynamic economy must have relative pay adjustments. But it is unwise to ask too much too quickly, especially of workers with a strong trade-union tradition and a powerful organization. The major unofficial strikes which accompanied the last two coalmining settlements led me many months ago to believe that something like the present situation was inevitable unless the case for exceptional treatment was fully and independently investigated before a breakdown of negotiations.

Members of the Court of Inquiry seemed eager to hear more from Hugh Clegg.

GARNETT: You have given a number of reasons why this case should be treated as an exceptional case. Have you any other thoughts as to what other exceptional factors there might be in the case of the miners?

CLEGG: I think I have set down all the factors I can think of which affect the miners. The combination of a new pay structure which very largely transfers them on to time rates and therefore means their rates have much more influence over their total earnings than is the case with most other workers, and the fact that they work for a nationalized industry has, over a period of rapid inflation, produced this result.

GARNETT: You make an exception in the case of the mineworkers and you do not think this will result in other pay increases; but at the time of the Guillebaud Report there were times when people thought that the argument about parity was disastrous and it did creep in and did take some killing.

CLEGG: It is true you can have formulae for settling pay. The Prices and Incomes Board brought several cases to the attention of the public where one pay increase in one case fed across to another case and created a pay increase and then fed back again, resulting in a ridiculous situation. Following the Guillebaud Report there were an increasing number of pay systems in the public service which based themselves on comparisons one with another and it did have this effect. Nevertheless, it is true that the Guillebaud increases raised the level of the railwaymen's pay in relation to that of other workers and sustained it there. If the whole benefit had been lost by comparative increases elsewhere, then they would not have improved their position over a period of time sufficient to allow for the other increases, but they did. It may be the case that one requires some carefully balanced incomes policy to get the full benefit of comparative pay increases, but even at that time when there was not such a policy it is clear that much of the benefit remained with those who had not intended to benefit from this.

CHAIRMAN: I would like to follow this up because I think this is a crucial point. Can you isolate the characteristics which must be found for that situation to occur? There are some cases where one increase is followed by another and nothing is gained. You give instances in your paper where special treatment in exceptional cases has enabled the gain to be maintained, so one would like to put one's finger on the circumstances and factors which give rise to these exceptional cases in order to see whether this is one such case.

CLEGG: It is easier to be sure of the facts than to be confident about the reasons for them. My guess would be that this is because it has been generally recognized by the public and by both sides of industry that what has been done in this case has to be regarded as the treatment of an exceptional case where a group of workers or an industry has been too low-paid. I think it was brought home by the events leading up to the Guillebaud Committee, Inquiry and Report that there was a case of low pay, and the exceptional increase therefore was not used generally in other industries as an argument for increasing their pay by like amounts. I would have thought that the same thing happened in the case of the Phelps-Brown increase to London busmen. Since the circumstances of those two cases have a lot in common with the current situation in the coal-mining industry I would be optimistic that if there were an exceptional pay increase here the same situation would apply.

CHAIRMAN: Would you agree or not agree that unions and those who represent unions are now, in 1972, much more skilful and determined in invoking increases in pay in other industries and drawing comparisons between them and using those comparisons to advance their claims than they were, say, in 1958 at the time of Guillebaud?

CLEGG: I am not sure I would want to say that present union leaders are more skilful than their predecessors even in the mining industry, but I think it is the case that pay claims have always been largely based on comparisons. At any rate, that has been true throughout the period I have been studying industrial relations, which goes back almost to the war. It was therefore true in the 1950s. I think it is true that the arguments that are used have changed a lot today and people are more aware of the need to think of comparisons in terms of earnings and rates and to realize that the two may not give the same results, but if that is true then it might now be said that people are more willing to accept the exceptional case of an industry like the mining industry than they were at the time of the Guillebaud Report, when there was a great deal more confusion in everybody's mind about the crucial distinction between basic rates and earnings and the way in which, in different industries and occupations, they can move badly out of step.

HUNTER: In the paper you make reference to outside analogues. Are you submitting that outside analogues are particularly appropriate in this case, and, if so, which are the analogues you want to look at?

CLEGG: I was not suggesting they were appropriate in this case and I would have got myself into a wonderful trap if I had suggested they were. I am saying that one of the reasons why the trouble has been confined to certain sectors of public employees is because other areas of public employees have been protected against anything like this happening to them. It is obvious that if a given occupation in the public service has a very great deal in common with a similar occupation outside you can give this protection by saying, 'The average pay inside the public service should be the same or very similar to the analogues outside the public service.' Nothing like that can be done for the mining industry directly. I am not sure I would want to advocate that it would have been very much in the miners' interest if it had been proposed a few years ago that their average earnings should be pegged to any particular figure of average earnings in respect of a group of industries or the economy outside. I am not sure that would have been wise, although, as you know, certain formulae were found to do something like this for the railway workers and London busmen at one time. I think some means have to be found of protecting workers in this sort of instance and I think the real protection is for everybody to understand exactly what is happening and to pay attention to this in their negotiations. When people have dropped badly behind something has to be done to pull them back into line before they come with the whip to put themselves in line.

CHAIRMAN: Of course, in the case of the mineworkers one does not have this comparability on which to base one's argument, and where that pushes one I am not sure.

CLEGG: I do see the difficulty and I am glad it is not mine in the circumstances. I think one has to have a rough and ready idea of what makes sense and what should be acceptable. As I say, I was taking the slip in average earnings in the coalmining industry compared with outside, and it is clear that too much has been asked of the mineworkers. What exactly would be needed to put them in a position where this was no longer true is obviously a very difficult judgement that someone has to make.

CHAIRMAN: The 1966 agreement was something with which the union went along and it was a negotiated settlement. It was a planned thing which was due to come to an end at the end of 1971 and it was then anticipated that there would be some sort of major surge forward. You make the point that 'a dynamic economy must have relative pay adjustments. But it is unwise to ask too much too quickly. . . .' I wondered whether, if it is said it is going down, the other side of the coin is relevant, that one should not try to go up too quickly. Would you agree with that?

CLEGG: Yes. I do not believe anybody negotiating in 1966 could possibly have foreseen the very rapid rate of inflation and the rapid increase in earnings which have put the miners in the position they are now in, given the agreement they then signed. Had the Power Loading Agreement been signed in a period of stable prices or slowly rising prices with earnings rising at a moderate pace, then, perhaps, the miners would not have experienced what they have experienced. The problem is that the miners as well as other people have shifted from piecework to timework in recent years. Other people have been caught in the same way, but nowhere else is there such a large body of workers in this position.

CHAIRMAN: It has been said this is a situation which has been developing over a five-year period and one could see it coming to an end and one knew one had to make plans for the future. With your experience of industrial relations I wondered what recommendations you would make to any party who recognized that this kind of step had to go. Do you see this as something to be achieved in the short term or something which could be explored by consultation or in terms of long-term plans?

CLEGG: Are you asking me what should have been done in 1966 or what should be done now?

CHAIRMAN: What perhaps might have been done at the beginning of 1971 when it was known this particular period was coming to an end and there was going to be this next step forward?

CLEGG: I would have thought it would be very difficult to say what ought to be the further adjustments within the mine-workers' pay structure. What seems to be clear is that they have been, as an industry, held back too much, and initially there should be in my view a considerable injection of additional pay through the industry as a whole to make the consequences of the agreement, the Power Loading Agreement, which I think was a very fine agreement in itself, more palatable and allow the industry to go on further to establish whatever advances it subsequently wishes to make. That is the first step in my view.

CHAIRMAN: I wonder if the Coal Board representatives want to ask any questions?

MILLIGAN*: Professor Clegg, in your general dissertation you mentioned particularly the railway industry as a special case because it was low-paid at the time of the Guillebaud Inquiry. I fully accept that that was then the situation. I want to ask: was it not also the case that there was a special situation in the railway industry in the conciliation grades at that time in that the difference between the lowest-grade rate and the highest-grade rate within the conciliation grades was very tight and the concertina between the bottom and the top was a very small one?

* J. Gordon Milligan is a member of the NCB.

CLEGG: I cannot honestly remember the figures, but I think in general the difficulty was that there were too many grades and the distance between the top and bottom was not necessarily very different from that in a number of other industries. However, they had squeezed within that distance so many grades that the differential between one grade and the next was sometimes ridiculous and was sometimes as little as 1s. or 2s. a week. But I do not think the distance from top to bottom was anything very different from that in other industries.

CHAIRMAN: I would like to thank you very much for your paper, Professor Clegg. It has gained everything by being brief and clear and we shall give it a great deal of thought.

Laurance Hunter later asked G. Clifford Shephard (NCB) for his views on some of Professor Clegg's arguments.

HUNTER: Could I turn back to the National Power Loading Agreement and refer to something which Professor Clegg mentioned yesterday? I would like to have your comments on these passages in his written statement: 'One consequence of the Power Loading Agreement was to hold back the pay of most face workers in relation to the rest of the industry, and to hold back the pay of some groups of face workers far more than others.' Is that something with which you would agree?

SHEPHARD: Yes.

HUNTER: 'It is, I believe, generally agreed by practitioners of industrial relations that, when a new pay structure alters the relative pay of groups of workers in an industry or undertaking, there is need for a generous overall increase to be injected, so that all, or all but a few, of the workers who suffer a relative setback should, nevertheless, receive a net advance.' The point I am making is that it does seem rather unusual, when a major revision of the wage structure is taking place, that workers should actually suffer a reduction in their monetary earnings. There are usual procedures like red-circle rates or guarantees to workers until the level of wages moves up the lowest-paid to their normal increase. In this case I understand that workers were obliged to accept a reduction in earnings.

SHEPHARD: As regards the three structures, the investment in money that the Board placed in acquiring the National Power Loading Agreement structure in 1966 was, I think, £5·5 million per annum. I understand that in introducing the third structure we contributed £2·5 million per annum and as regards the craft structure our contribution was £1·5 million per annum, but with this additional injection of money in fact there was not a complete overtake; it did not result in the position where every man was in receipt of an increase under those three agreements and did not provide that kind of cushion.

HUNTER: What I am suggesting is that this is fairly unusual.

DALY: Unique.

SHEPHARD: In my view it is unusual in the climate of today, the climate of industrial relations and wages aspirations today.

HUNTER: Do you mean today or are you speaking in the context of the last five or six years during which time a lot of productivity deals have been gone through?

SHEPHARD: In the context of the last three years.

GARNETT: In my experience it is an incredible achievement, but the question arises: how was this brought about? Perhaps the situation we are dealing with at the moment, as Professor Clegg suggested, dates back to this period, but how was it possible to achieve this in the coal industry, because it has never been achieved anywhere else in this country?

SHEPHARD: I have to pay tribute to the trade union side in recognizing that if people are going to move up with such a structure then other people are going to move more slowly. I pay tribute to the National Union of Mineworkers for their support and courageous tackling of this situation over the years.

GARNETT: I still do not understand why the men accepted this situation. No other men have accepted the situation. I understand the logic that if some go up some go down, but how was this achieved? What was the special circumstance of coal which permitted you to achieve that which could not be achieved elsewhere?

SHEPHARD: A substantial number of men were being brought up and a minority of men, particularly in Kent and Nottinghamshire, were not going up at anything like the same pace.

The NCB did not seriously reply to this question, but subsequently Lawrence Daly took up the theme.

DALY: The question was asked by the Court as to how it was possible to put through the reform which involved thousands of miners – many of them substantially – in what can only be described as many thousands of pounds in wages loss. I am going to claim it was due to the fact that in the mining communities there is a powerful egalitarian tradition. I have never heard any miner question the fact (certainly not a single area of the union that I can recall at any conference since nationalization) or raise the matter or suggest that it should be changed, that the mineworker who is higher-paid takes during his holidays a lower rate than his earnings, in order to give the same rate of holiday pay to one who is perhaps lower-paid. This is something I would think would be very much questioned in many other industries. It just never is questioned in the mining industry. This is basically why we have been able to get a majority of our membership to move towards the concept of uniform day rates, even though it has meant a substantial minority of actual reduction, or reductions in terms of real earnings, because of the very small increases they received while we were approaching parity. These men, even where they disagreed, at the end of the day, loyally accepted the majority decisions through the democratic procedures of the union.

I am not saying that many of them were happy about it, but at least they belonged to a basically democratic organization and they accepted the majority decisions, often at a great deal of expense to themselves and their families.

William Campbell Adamson later presented evidence on behalf of the CBI based on a different viewpoint from Hugh Clegg's.

CAMPBELL ADAMSON: We are extremely concerned not, of course, to argue the technical issue of the case – that is not our business and we are not qualified to do it. We should like to bring the Court's attention to the effect we think it might have on the future rate of inflation, a rate which is still the highest of all the western developed countries but which is considerably lower than it was. I mean the effect that a very high settlement might have on other settlements and therefore on the ability or inability of industry to resist fairly heavy price increases at the end of the period.

I should like to make one more point. We have not in this country to my mind, unfortunately, got any sort of a system which attempts to evaluate the level of wages and salaries across the country as a whole. There are many deserving cases which many people would think are out of line.

We exist on a system of voluntary collective bargaining, built up over many years. One of the things we know well from experience is that in a system of voluntary collective bargaining, particularly in recent years, both sides have been very much influenced by what was the going rate at the time and are very naturally willing to quote high settlements made in other areas. It is this, therefore, that worries us when we think about the large number of claims in the private sector that are due to be negotiated in the next month.

If this is the case, and if it makes it impossible to continue the downward albeit slow level of settlements in money terms, then we are almost bound to find ourselves, we feel, with the last year's work undone and a grave rate of inflation again. We feel that a growing rate of inflation, and inflation getting out of hand, again would be as damaging to all the people who work in industry as it is to industrial investment and to future competitiveness. Further, we believe it would make more difficult the pulling down of the rate of unemployment, which we deplore and which we want to pull down. Because there is no doubt in our minds that the rate of unemployment at the present time, with the shaking out that has gone on, is closely connected with agreements in the past of levels of wages which are out of proportion to the increase in productivity.

These are the main facts which we wanted to bring to the Court of Inquiry's attention. We are not, as you see, discussing in any way whether the miners should be a special case or not. All we are saying is that we hope the Court will take into account what we think will be the dangerous effects of an over-high settlement in this industry, the economy as a whole, and on the people who work in industry, on our future possibility as management to increase real wages and to increase profitability and competitiveness.

John Hughes, of the Trade Union Research Unit, challenged William Campbell Adamson.

HUGHES: In your written submission, you say: 'If it were decided that the coalmining dispute should be regarded as a special case and an exceptionally high increase conceded, this would clearly make it difficult for employers involved in forthcoming negotiations to secure settlements which would continue the downward trend. Industrial experience shows that individual pay settlements are repeatedly determined not by any consideration of the position within the company or by productivity considerations, but by comparability and the concept of the going rate.' That is your position?

CAMPBELL ADAMSON: Yes.

HUGHES: Have you read the evidence of Professor Clegg?

CAMPBELL ADAMSON: I read a little bit in the press this morning.

HUGHES: Could I ask you your view of this section of Professor Clegg's evidence which is exactly contrary to what you have just in your own evidence put forward? Professor Clegg had this to say: 'It is sometimes said that it would be self-defeating to raise the miners' pay by x per cent above the original offer because subsequent settlements elsewhere would then be x per cent higher than otherwise, until at the end of twelve months the original relationships would be restored, and prices would meanwhile also have risen by x per cent or thereabouts.' That is really very much what you are saying. Professor Clegg went on to say: 'However, the evidence of past instances of special treatment for exceptional cases points in the other direction. It has proved possible to achieve lasting remedies for maladjustments in pay.' I would ask whether the CBI has made any study of this question, because it appears very clear that Professor Clegg, from his experience, is arguing the exact contrary to the CBI?

CAMPBELL ADAMSON: I think this is a question of experience. As far as I know, Professor Clegg is an academic who has made a very considerable study of this; he has also had practical experience on boards and courts of inquiry. As far as I know, Professor Clegg has not – although I may be wrong – been in the practical situation of down-to-earth negotiations at plant or company level. I have myself spent all my life, with the exception of the last three years, in industry. Many of our members, who are living with this all the time, agree with me. In seeking to attempt to put forward a few facts, this can only be based on practical experience. It is very easy to refute it. It is very easy to say that when future claims arise, this will be considered purely as a special case. I suspect that there will be other cases which can rightly be regarded as special. I therefore am worried about the effects.

HUGHES: Does that mean then that the CBI is reluctant to see industries, public corporations, pursuing the reform of pay systems?

CAMPBELL ADAMSON: Absolutely to the contrary.

HUGHES: If the CBI wants to see firms and public corporations pursuing the reform of pay systems, do they think that the employers negotiating those reforms of pay systems should make it worthwhile for their labour force to accept those changes?

CAMPBELL ADAMSON: Certainly. We are talking here, as I understand it, of a whole industry, with offers in public having already been made, for the three categories of labour. We are not, as far as I know, talking about a complete change in the structure.

HUGHES: I do not know if you have studied the reform of the pay system of the mining industry in the 1960s?

CAMPBELL ADAMSON: No, not very much.

HUGHES: I do not think the Coal Board would want to disagree with the NUM side in saying there has been a major reform, historically probably the most important reform in the pay system that the industry has ever seen. It was a pay reform which has eliminated piecework; it eliminated all the inflationary consequences of piecework and has basically introduced measured timework. If the Board disagree, then they can. Do you think the miners deserve some reward for the acceptance of that reformed pay system?

CAMPBELL ADAMSON: Certainly.

HUGHES: What you are saying is the miners certainly deserved a reward for that reform and that would therefore be an exceptional circumstance justifying a review of pay?

CAMPBELL ADAMSON: As I understand it, we are talking about a claim properly made by the NUM for the industry as a whole. We are not, as I understand it, talking here about a complete reform of the pay structure.

HUGHES: We are talking about a situation in which that reform of the pay system has gone through over the last six years and is now virtually complete?

CAMPBELL ADAMSON: We are talking also surely about a reform gone through which has been negotiated at each turn and which has therefore been agreed and accepted as a result of those reforms.

HUGHES: Can I just explain we are looking at a situation after carrying through a pay reform which has taken six years, and we have put before this Court very extensive evidence of a very severe relative decline in the position of miners over precisely the same period. Would you like to comment?

CAMPBELL ADAMSON: Only that again, as I understand it, the offers already made up to the latest public offer would have changed the position, the relative position, of the mineworkers in this country. I said at the outset that I was not here to argue. I was not here to argue about the technicalities of the mineworkers' case. I am not in a position to do so.

12 The NUM Sums Up

We are not going to use our final statement for any rhetorical appeals to this Court. We have submitted a great mass of directly relevant evidence that fully substantiates our claim. The Court knows that its job is to consider facts, and we have provided those facts.

The one thing we can say with certainty is that the more the Court studies our evidence the more they must be impressed by the justice of the wage claim we have made of £35 for five days' underground work involving the highest degree of skill, effort, responsibility and exposure to danger. We could rightly and reasonably have asked for more for these men.

But, as our evidence has shown, there is an immense degree of social responsibility in the mining community. Our union is concerned to give due priority to the lowest-paid.

We do, however, want to emphasize a point that has been implicit in all our evidence but should now be made very clearly and explicitly. From the mid-1960s through to 1971 the mining industry was carrying through the most important reform of pay systems in its history. We have shown that there has been a direct connection between that reform and the relative (and absolute) decline in miners' earnings.

We take the view that this is the exact *opposite* of what should have come about. In all logic, there should have been some reward for our active cooperation in going over to a reformed pay system. Instead, we were penalized.

This is hardly a good advertisement for the replacement of payment-by-results systems by measured task work in other industries. Why should workers and their trade unions cooperate in the reform of pay systems if the result is a worsening of their pay position?

The new payment system in mining *is* a genuine reform. It is much less dispute-prone than the earlier pay system (I know this sounds odd in view of our strike. But the *incidence* of strikes has fallen abruptly. It is the *level* of our pay that has caused the present industrial unrest. The pay *system* has sharply reduced local strike action.) It also enables better planning of manpower use and labour costs.

Therefore, there should have been real pay benefits for miners as a reward for pay reform. That is what, for example, motor-car workers have been securing, and rightly securing, as they negotiate the move from piecework to measured daywork. That is what miners should have secured – and should now be given.

We have another strong ground for saying that our relative position should have *improved* in recent years instead of deteriorating.

We have shown the miners' contribution to improved productivity in the last decade. We have shown how dramatic has been the rise in productivity – and this in what the economists call a 'diminishing returns' industry. Compared with ten years earlier, the miner in 1970 was producing one hundred and fifty tons more coal each year. There would have been some difficulty in bringing one hundred and fifty tons of coal to this room, but if we had done so we would have been able to impress clearly upon you what these abstract figures of productivity really mean.

So we ask that our contribution over a long period to increased productivity be properly recognized.

The Wilberforce Inquiry Report on the Electricity Supply Dispute (Cmnd 4594) dealt with the similar record of active cooperation in productivity advance by electricity-supply workers during the 1960s. A parallel situation. It said:

We concluded that over the period since 1965 the industrial staff in the industry have cooperated in major changes in working practices and conditions which have facilitated the effective use of the large capital-investment programme, have contributed to a far more effective use of manpower, and have made possible a reduction of nearly 20 per cent in the industrial labour force in the past three years.

We agree with the NBPI that workers who have contributed so

greatly ought not to see their earnings increase at a rate slower than other workers in industry; and indeed we believe that . . . the level of earnings of the industrial staff in electricity should have risen more than the average for manual workers in industry and public service, many of whom have not, in this period, made anything like so large a contribution (page 41, paragraphs 12.2 and 12.3).

We endorse that view. We agree that instead of falling further behind in relative terms, that kind of cooperation in productivity requires an improvement in relative terms.

So our case reaches this far. In the name of equity, of fair dealing, there were no reasons why men in our industry should have fallen back in relative terms as compared with workers in other industries.

There are, in fact, two powerful reasons why they should have advanced more rapidly:

1. Acceptance of a radically reformed pay structure. (Of course, historically, it was more than mere acceptence; it was the union that fought for this reform, fought for an end to anomalies, fought for the principle of the rate for the job.)

2. Active cooperation in sustained increases in productivity under arduous and testing conditions.

We say this. Our case more than justifies the pay demands we put forward. Our pay demands do not begin to compensate miners for what they have lost during recent years as a result of the relative decline in their earnings. That decline was unjustified.

Nor do our demands go very far beyond checking and partly reversing the deterioration in our relative position over recent years. We could reasonably – in terms of accepted bargaining arguments – have asked for increases that would mean our earnings rising considerably more since the mid-1960s than the earnings of other workers.

Instead, we have been moderate. We have not sought any excessive or unreasonable advance. But we do now demand the rates that have been put forward in our claim. . . .

Can we recall finally one aspect of our evidence? We represent 280,000 workers. We put several of them before you as witnesses yesterday. We could have called many more. We ask you in compiling your report to remember above all from our evidence what those men had to tell you. Remember that the detailed statistics we presented are about those people and their human needs. Those men, giving their actual evidence yesterday, were telling you one thing above all. A great industrial injustice has been done to them, and to their colleagues.

It is your task to end that injustice.

If the nation gives the miners justice, then the miners – in the future as in the past – will give of their best to the country.

Report of a Court of Inquiry into a Dispute between the National Coal Board and the National Union of Mineworkers under the Chairmanship of the Rt Hon Lord Wilberforce*

To the Right Honourable the Secretary of State for Employment

Sir,

We were appointed by you on 11 February 1972, with the following terms of reference:

To inquire into the causes and circumstances of the present dispute between the National Coal Board and members of the National Union of Mineworkers and to report.

In accordance with the terms of our appointment we submit the following Report.

Introduction

1. We met in London on 13 February 1972, to discuss the arrangements for the hearing. We sat in public in London on 15 and 16 February 1972, to hear the evidence and submissions of the parties and the CBI. We also met in private to consider our Report.

2. At the hearings the case for the NUM was presented by Mr L. Daly, the General Secretary. The case for the NCB was presented by Mr D. J. Ezra, the Chairman. Mr W. O. Campbell Adamson gave evidence on behalf of the CBI. The TUC were invited to give evidence but did not think this necessary.

The following abbreviations are used in this Report:

NCB National Coal Board
NUM National Union of Mineworkers
NPLA National Power Loading Agreement

*HMSO, February 1972, Cmnd 4903

3. The circumstances of the dispute are well known. The NUM submitted a claim to the NCB on 20 July 1971, the principal clause of which sought to establish a weekly minimum wage of £26 surface, £28 underground and £35 under the National Power Loading Agreement. These figures represented increases of £8, £9 and £5 respectively. The Board on 12 October 1971 offered an increase of £1.80 per week for the minimum surface grade and £1.75 for all other grades. This offer was rejected. There followed an overtime ban and a ballot in which 58·8 per cent voted in favour of strike action.

4. Improved offers were made by the Board before the strike, the most significant on 4 January 1972, covering some improvements in the money offered, five additional rest days, and a productivity deal. This was rejected and the strike commenced on 9 January.

5. On 9 February the Secretary of State for Employment met the two sides after which further negotiations took place under the auspices of the Department's conciliation officers. As a result of these further talks the NCB made a further offer which would have given £3 to surface workers, giving a basic minimum rate of £21 but with minimum guaranteed earnings for five days of £22; £3.50 to underground workers given a new basic minimum of £22.50; and £2.75 to face workers raising the National Power Loading Agreement rate to £32.75. The offer would operate from the date of resumption of work and would last eighteen months from then.

6. The offer was rejected by the NUM Executive and when the talks were resumed on 10 February the NUM made it clear that the offer was not adequate but that they would consider £6 for surface workers, £7 for underground workers and £4 for power loaders, plus an additional week's holiday. They also wanted the agreement to operate from 1 November 1971. The NCB were unable to contemplate a settlement of this size.

7. Negotiations therefore came to an end and the Secretary of State told the parties that he proposed to appoint a Court of Inquiry. By the time the Court was set up, Emergency Powers had been taken. Severe power cuts ensued, with many workers laid off.

8. In this critical situation we have decided that we should

concentrate attention on producing our Report with more than normal urgency. Consequently we have excluded any detailed description of the history of the dispute and the wage structure and omitted a summary of the evidence of the parties. This is no reflection on the value we attach to the very full written and oral submissions but rather an indication of our recognition of the urgency of the task.

The special circumstances of the miners' case

9. The NUM stressed in its evidence to us the past contribution made by the coalmining industry to the national economy and submitted that the environment in which men worked in coalmining and coking justified that its membership should rank among the highest-paid industrial workers in Britain. Working conditions in coalmines are certainly among the toughest and least attractive, and we agree that miners' pay levels should recognize this. In addition, as many underground workers have to be redeployed on surface work (which attracts comparatively lower pay than underground work) because their health has been adversely affected by working conditions underground, we think that equity requires that pay levels for surface work need also to be improved.

10. The British coalmining community is in some ways quite unique. Coalminers and their families often live in poor housing in isolated communities where coalmining is a traditional and sometimes the only way of life. There is a strong egalitarian feeling among the men, which manifests itself in their concern for the lower-paid men in the industry. One example of this is the industry's long standing arrangement that holiday pay is not calculated on an individual worker's usual earnings, but on the average pay of the workforce. The miner's concern for his fellow men has been reflected in the role which his union has played in attempting to resolve the many difficult problems which have faced his industry since nationalization.

11. Since about 1957, when falling demand caused undistributed coal stocks to rise dramatically, the miners have wholeheartedly cooperated in a continuing programme of streamlining coal production. In that period they have seen their numbers working in pits reduced from over 700,000 to under 290,000 and

the number of producing collieries fall from over eight hundred to under three hundred. This rundown, which was brought about with the cooperation of the miners and of their union, is without parallel in British industry in terms of the social and economic costs it has inevitably entailed for the mining community as a whole.

12. During this period of concentrating production on fewer collieries, production methods became highly mechanized and the miners responded by learning new skills and by cooperating with the NCB in the further concentration of production on faces where machines could be used to the best advantage. This policy of concentration enabled productivity to rise year by year. In 1957 output per manshift stood at under 25 cwt; by 1971 it had climbed to 44·2 cwt, an increase of 77·5 per cent. In some years there were marked increases in productivity, particularly in the period 1967–8 and 1968–9, when the percentage increases on the previous year's were 6·7 and 9·0 respectively. While the difficulty of identifying the specific contribution of labour in such circumstances has long been recognized, there can be no doubt that the productivity increases achieved reflect much credit on both men and colliery managements.

13. The reduction in the numbers of men employed in collieries, together with the programme of concentration of production, has had far-reaching effects upon individual mining communities. Where pits have been closed, many men now have further to travel to work, as alternative employment opportunities are often not available. Additionally, large numbers of men have had to move home, in some cases more than once.

14. Yet the men continued to cooperate with the NCB in its efforts to secure a viable future for the industry in the face of increasing competition from other fuels. In 1971 the NUM and the NCB completed a phased programme of restructuring the industry's wage system which they had begun in 1955. This programme substituted a daywage system of national rates for the previous system of local piece rates. The NUM had long desired to remove regional differentials on grounds of equity. It had also objected to a piecework system of payment because geological conditions often resulted in an inverse relationship between output and effort. The NCB for its part had aimed to reduce dis-

putes and control wage drift by removing wage bargaining from pit and area level to the national level.

15. The introduction of daywages led to a big reduction in the number of local wage disputes and this in turn released colliery managers to spend more time on improving production. It also enabled management to maintain closer control of wage differentials, manning levels and deployment, which had previously often been the subject of disputes. In particular, the removal of wage drift resulting from local bargaining meant that the NCB had a more effective means of controlling wage costs in the industry.

16. The new day-rate system of miners' pay discourages the wage drift seen in other industries. A position has now been reached whereby their basic rates constitute a higher proportion of total earnings than is usual. According to the Department of Employment's New Earnings Survey of 1970, underground workers' basic pay in April 1970 amounted to more than four-fifths of total pay, whereas in all production industries as much as one-third of earnings comes from sources other than basic rates. This special position of mineworkers' basic rates, together with other special factors which we have described above, resulted in the whole labour force of the industry suffering a loss in relative terms as compared with other industrial workers. This deterioration in the mineworkers' relative position can be demonstrated in terms of relative movements in the earnings league.

17. A major element in the case centres on the drastic change in the relative position of the mineworkers in the national pay structure. During most of the post-war period until 1965, the mineworker had consistently been near the top of the payment structure, and this was no doubt a reflection of the arduous and hazardous character of the job and the importance of his contribution to national production. During the period 1965 to 1970 – the very period when the revision of the wage structure was being implemented – the pay of the miner fell from near the top rank to a level in the middle of the structure. Undoubtedly this was attributable in considerable measure to the growing importance of basic pay as a constituent of gross earnings while the overall earnings structure in the industry was moving ahead rather less quickly than elsewhere. From a position in which

Table A Movement in the relative weekly earnings of full-time men employed in coalmining

Industry group	Time									
	October 1960		October 1965		October 1968		October 1970		October 1971	
	Average weekly earnings	Rank*	Average weekly earnings	Rank*	Average weekly earnings	Rank*	Average weekly earnings	Rank*	Average weekly earnings	Rank*
Manufacturing	£15.16	—	£20.16	—	£22.82‡	—	£28.91	—	£31.36†	—
Coalmining	£16.28	3rd	£21.21	3rd	£24.12	5th	£28.01	12th	£31.65	9th
Coalmining as a ratio of manufacturing	107·4	—	105·2	—	105·7‡	—	96·9	—	100·9	—

* Out of 21 industry groups.
† This figure is undoubtedly biased downwards because of the depressed situation of the manufacturing industry at this time.
‡ These figures are incorrect. They should read £23.62 and 102·1 (Eds.).

average weekly earnings in coalmining had stood well above average earnings in manufacturing industry, the industry found itself in 1971 in the reverse situation where its workers earned substantially less, on average, than those in manufacturing. The precise dimensions of the relative decline vary according to the statistical series on pay that is used, and the base date that is chosen for comparison. However, after careful study of a variety of alternative measures and base dates, we have been able to draw no conclusion other than that a serious fall has occurred in the relative pay position of the mineworkers, when compared with those in manufacturing industry.

18. Table A indicates the decline, but the figures can be no more than illustrative for the reasons given. The apparent recovery of some lost ground in 1971 is partly to be explained by the 1970 settlement in coalmining which favoured some low-paid workers, and also by the fact that earnings in manufacturing in October 1971 were depressed below trend by the recession in business conditions.

19. We have not reached our decision on the basis of this Table alone since more and less favourable statistics may be produced, nor have we quantified our recommendations for increases in coalmining pay by an exact formula derived from relative wage indices. We have, however, formed an impression of the position in the national pay structure which seems appropriate for the industry and we have attempted to reflect that in our recommendations.

20. This is not to say that we take the view that the relative wage position of any industry should be immutable. Some changes are necessary from time to time as economic circumstances, technology and other factors alter. In our view, however, the fall in the ranking of coalmining pay has been quite unwarranted by any such changes and we have tried to provide a fresh evaluation of the relativities and seek to implement that assessment by our recommendations.

21. One further point deserves attention, that of the distribution of earnings in the industry. We observed that an effort had been made by the NCB in 1970 to improve the position of the low-paid worker, and there is no doubt that some workers have fared rather better than others in the implementation of the new

wage structure. The fact remains that a significant proportion of the industry's workforce, before the last negotiations commenced, still fell into the category of lower-paid workers, while, as explained in the next section, others at the upper end of the scale had experienced reductions in their money earnings for identical work. These aspects have been reflected in our recommendations.

22. The programme of change in the industry's wage structure (1955–71), particularly the National Power Loading Agreement of 1966 and the Third Daywage Structure Agreement of 1971, was carried through jointly by the NCB and the NUM but considerable sacrifices were called for by some of the men. We would like to refer to some significant figures – these are illustrative, not exhaustive.

1. The National Power Loading Agreement of 1966 introduced a national rate of pay in place of pit and district agreements covering workers on mechanized faces. The national rate was not applied all at once; the Nottinghamshire rate (the second highest) was taken as the standard, and rates for other districts were to be brought up to it by 31 December 1971. This meant that, in the years 1966–71, the higher-rated districts received smaller increases in pay than those which, in 1966, were at the lowest level (e.g. Scotland, Durham, South Wales). Even these latter received increases which involved a small decline in real earnings. In the case of the higher-rated districts the real decline was substantial. We are sure that these effects were not intended; they were the consequence of the decline in purchasing power in the years following 1966.

2. As a result of this uneven adjustment of wage rates from 1966 onwards, a number of men suffered not merely a real decrease in earnings, but a decrease in money terms. The NUM provided a statistical table showing this effect in relation to the Third National Daywage Structure which became effective in June 1971. The real impact on this in human terms was brought home to us by the evidence of three witnesses called by the NUM.

(a) Mr Jack Collins is a miner working in such exceptionally hot conditions that men work naked. He receives £5 a shift under the

Third Daywage Structure Agreement, whereas in 1963 he was getting £5 10s. a shift. He is away from home ten hours a day.

(b) Mr Peter Lippiat in 1967 was at a power-loader face at 86s. 9d. per shift. In 1968 he went to a contract face and earned between 110s. and 120s. per shift. In 1969 he went back to a power-loader face at 92s. 1d. a shift and is now at the £30 rate for five shifts.

(c) Mr James O'Connor, as a result of coming under power loading, lost £5 per week.

23. We are sure that these examples can be multiplied. They reflect, in our opinion, an exceptional situation, which could only have come about and been accepted, as a result of exceptional restraint. In retrospect it now seems clear that too much was asked of men as the price of the new wages structure.

24. We agree with Professor Clegg when he said in relation to this situation that:

One consequence of the Power Loading Agreement was to hold back the pay of most face workers in relation to the rest of the industry, and to hold back the pay of some groups of face workers far more than others. It is, I believe, generally agreed by practitioners of industrial relations that, when a new pay structure alters the relative pay of groups of workers in an industry or undertaking, there is need for a generous over-all increase to be injected, so that all, or all but a few of, the workers who suffer a relative setback should, nevertheless, receive a net advance. But over the last few years a large number of miners have been asked to take a reduction relative to the general level of miners' earnings at a time when that general level has been falling behind the movement of pay in the country as a whole.

25. In our opinion this is a special and powerful factor underlying the present unrest and calling for adjustment.

The ability to pay

26. Accepting that special consideration needs to be given to the mineworkers' case, we now turn to examine the NCB's ability to pay. The NUM's original claim has been costed at about £120 million for a full year and a revised claim at about £100 million. These figures include repercussive costs likely to be incurred in respect of the pay of other NCB employees whose pay is traditionally related to that of the mineworkers themselves.

27. The present financial objective, agreed with the Government, is to break even in each year. Nevertheless, the NCB began 1971–2 with a cumulative deficit of nearly £35 million.

28. The NUM has claimed that the NCB's ability to meet the claim is inhibited by the high levels of interest and depreciation charges that the industry has to bear. These together amounted to £90 million in 1970–71, an annual figure close to the union's revised claim. However, as explained in Appendix 2, two-thirds of this amount is attributable to depreciation (at original and not replacement costs). At best only £30 million could be found by saving on interest charges, assuming the whole of the outstanding capital debt was written off.

29. A second way of financing a major claim would be by a considerable price increase. The NCB estimates, however, that if sales were to be maintained at about the 140 million tons level, price increases would have to be held to a minimum and certainly less than 10 per cent. If prices were allowed to rise substantially in order to meet all possible costs arising from the NUM's claim, this would reduce the market by perhaps one-third with consequential reductions in the workforce, particularly in the 'peripheral' coalfields.

30. If, however, such a reduction in employment is quite unacceptable, then the Government will have to provide the necessary finance, because it is unreasonable to expect miners' wages to be held down to finance uneconomic operations.

31. We set out further details of this argument in Appendix 2.

Wider considerations

32. We have seen it as our duty to examine the circumstances in the coal industry over as wide an area as possible. We think it necessary to travel beyond a mere consideration of percentage increases of rates of pay or earnings and to look at the wage structure in the coal industry, its history and development, the economics of the industry, the conditions in which men work and the causes, so far as we can understand them, of underlying unrest among the miners. Of course the coal industry cannot be looked at in isolation. Although there are many factors bearing upon its size and prosperity which are beyond its control – and also beyond our powers to recommend policy – we have to think

of the industry as it exists in today's climate. Specifically, we cannot shut our eyes to the continuing danger of inflation, which presents the most serious threat to the standards of living of everyone, including the miners themselves. We bear firmly in mind the national interest, which requires the survival of a viable coal industry in competitive conditions, with a contented and efficient labour force.

33. We have tried, impartially, independently and urgently to bring these considerations into balance.

Conclusions

34. As an approach to our conclusions, we can sum up the main factors which have convinced us that the miners' claim should be given exceptional national treatment.

1. The surface workers who are on the minimum rate of £18 are among the lower-paid. Their opportunities for alternative work are limited because they may well live in isolated communities. In a number of cases they have suffered sickness and injury in the service of the mines.

2. The large group of men underground but not at the face do work which is heavy, dirty, hot and frequently cramped. In this day and age when physical conditions in other jobs have improved greatly the relative discomforts of working below ground become greater. Other occupations have their dangers and inconveniences, but we know of none in which there is such a combination of danger, health hazard, discomfort in working conditions, social inconvenience and community isolation.

3. The men working on the face and associated with the face, who are in key jobs winning coal, not only suffer the problems of other people below ground, but they may need to work in dust masks and suffer considerable noise and are at maximum danger risk.

4. There has been quite exceptional cooperation shown by miners in the last few years in moving from piecework schemes to day-working schemes in the interest of greater efficiency. This co-operation has been a model to industry as a whole. The consequences of this change in pay structure has been to hold back the pay of most face workers in relation to the rest of the industry, and

to hold back the pay of some groups of face workers far more than others, to the extent that some miners are now earning less than they were five years ago. It is normal in such cases elsewhere in industry at the time of major changes to the wage structure to inject a significant overall increase. No such injection has taken place in the case of the miners.

5. Shift payments are minimal or non-existent, which has advantages in terms of efficiency by giving greater flexibility in the organization of work.

35. It is for these reasons which are exceptional and do not apply in industry generally that we believe the mineworkers at this particular time have a just case for special treatment.

36. In the light of these factors we consider the figures relevant to the present claims for wage adjustment. In our view there are *two quite separate elements in any possible wage increase in this industry*.

37. First, there is what we may call the *periodic increase*, which is designed to take account of the cost of living and other considerations. We accept that for the present this is a fact of life and that negotiators on both sides expect that it will occur.

38. But, secondly, there is what we may call the *adjustment* factor. This means that a time may come in any industry when a distortion or trend has to be recognized as due for correction.

39. We are convinced, from the arguments we have stated, that the present is a time when a definite and substantial adjustment in wage levels is called for in the coal industry.

40. The existence of these two quite separate factors seems to us to have been overlooked until the present inquiry brought it to light. This explains the very large gap in the two sides' negotiating positions. The initial offers of the NCB were based on the 'annual round'; the NUM was demanding an upward adjustment to improve the relative standard of miners' pay.

41. The NCB's offers were, we consider, in the light of the objective seen by them, perfectly fair. They represented, roughly, an increase of some 7–9 per cent over the previous rates. They were carefully related to the NCB's ability to pay from current revenues, in accordance with their statutory duties. The miners' case, again, from their point of view, was logical. If their claims

exceeded, as we think they did, what could be regarded as a proper adjustment, they were squarely based on arguments which in principle we accept. It was because the miners felt that their special case was not being recognized in the negotiations that they came out on strike in the first place and remained out with increasing bitterness.

42. We think it an essential part of the present settlement that the miners' basic claim for a general and exceptional increase should be recognized. We believe that in general this is accepted by public opinion and if it cannot be paid for out of the NCB's revenue account, in accordance with its statutory obligations, we think that the public, through the Government, should accept the charge.

43. We recognize that by accepting the arguments for a re-assessment we are moving on to the difficult territory of placing a relative value upon different jobs. We are conscious of the difficulties of establishing any general principle, but we think that the need for a reassessment is clear and that it can be reasonably quantified in money terms.

44. Our suggested settlement, therefore, contains within it two separate elements, the periodic increase and the adjustment factor. We do not attempt to segregate them exactly, but we attach considerable importance to each. Together they make up the increases we now recommend. (These are summarized in Appendix 1.)

Recommendations
Surface workers

45. First we think it necessary substantially to increase the pay of surface workers. These include the men drawing the lowest pay of £18 a week before deductions. Some of these men have previously worked underground on higher wages and have been obliged through ill-health or injury to take work on the surface. We recommend an increase of £5, making a minimum rate of £23.

Underground workers

46. The next category is that of men in the same wage structure (1955 Daywage Structure) who work underground. They receive,

basically, the same as the first category, plus a differential because of working underground. This differential was fixed in 1955 at £1. We attach importance to this differential because of the rigours and discomforts involved; we recommend that it should be increased from £1 to £2. This makes the overall increase £6, bringing the minimum rate underground to £25.

Face workers

47. The third category is that of men covered by the NPLA plus those under the Third Daywage Structure (Grades A, B and C). It has been normal practice that whatever increase is given should apply equally to all these men – and without necessarily accepting the immutability of this, we see no reason to make a change at the present time. We think that an increase is called for, not only because of the continuing arduous character of these jobs but because it is these men, particularly the NPLA workers, who have been unevenly affected by the levelling of rates consequent on the revisions between 1966 and 1971. We recommend an increase of £4.50, which will give the NPLA men a minimum rate of £34.50.

Effective date and duration of settlement

48. We recommend that all these increases should be backdated to 1 November 1971 and should run for a period of sixteen months from that date, i.e. until 28 February 1973. An allowance for the duration of the settlement has been built in to the recommended figures. The length of time is indispensable to give all those in the mining industry long enough to bend their attention to increasing productivity rather than, within a few months, to be entering another phase of national negotiation. Four months of this period has already elapsed and in less than twelve months negotiations will again be in hand. The extra time may give a chance to all concerned to repair the damage done and get back to an efficient and viable industry with a secure future. The extra months also give time for the negotiation of the outstanding matters, including the productivity scheme, all of which should improve the working conditions of miners.

49. If it is thought advantageous to hold the periodic negotiation in November then there is nothing to prevent the parties getting back to this timing at the next settlement.

Other matters

50. There were two further aspects of the claim. The adult rate for all at the age of eighteen – this affects 17,000 people – and an increase in holidays. We do not propose to make recommendations on either of these matters, other than to urge the NCB and the NUM to complete their negotiations not later than 1 May 1972. In the case of extra holidays, they should so arrange that maximum productivity is achieved.

Productivity

51. It is only by improving productivity that any long-term increases in real wages can be obtained. Productivity in the industry has been steadily rising over the last fifteen years from 24·8 cwt per manshift to 44·2. This trend will need to continue and the NCB talked of an expected increase due to technical and mechanical improvements of 3·5 per cent a year, amounting to a potential of over 50 per cent in the next few years. The NUM did not disagree with these figures. There is also room for further increases in productivity due to still greater commitment of all those employed in the mines. The effective use of the machines and the reduction of absence depends to a considerable extent on the keenness and sense of urgency of the miners. The NUM stressed that if a just settlement can be reached miners would give of their best to their work. This potential good will is there to be tapped by managers, including supervisors.

52. In this industry, for reasons which the Court entirely supports, piecework earnings and other forms of fluctuating incentives have been removed, and there is therefore a particular need to improve face-to-face communication and leadership of the working group. The NCB have recognized this need by increasing supervisory training and by teach-ins before new faces are operated. Further attention should be given to the role of the Deputy, the size of the working group, and the systematic and regular use of discussion or briefing groups at all locations.

53. We heard from both the NCB and the NUM of their efforts to evolve a productivity payments scheme which would avoid returning to the disadvantages of piecework-type payments. Twenty schemes have been considered, but none found entirely satisfactory. The NCB and the NUM should commence dis-

cussion before the end of March to agree a scheme by September, which would reflect increases in productivity. The scheme should be agreed nationally, and could be based on increases in productivity nationally or by individual pits, or by a combination of the two.

Industrial relations

54. The fundamentally good industrial relations between the NCB and the NUM have already been commented on. In recent years the removal of piecework has reduced the number of local disputes, but lack of employment security remains a natural anxiety; pension provision and redundancy arrangements should be reviewed. At national level relationships appear to have deteriorated over the last two years and this has not been helped by the present long-drawn-out struggle. All those in the mining industry are receiving exceptional treatment in the interests of the nation as a whole. It is important that leaders of both sides realize the trust that has been put in them and by early discussion find means of avoiding the present type of dispute with its damage to the nation. If they do not consider their arbitration machinery satisfactory, then they must evolve some new machinery. The argument is not accepted that arbitration machinery cannot be independent and make judgements based on justice.

55. We wish to record our sincere gratitude to our Secretary, Mrs J. M. Collingridge, our Assistant Secretary, Mr D. Bower, and the other staff at the Office of Manpower Economics. All of them worked unsparingly for very long hours so that our Report could be produced with all the rapidity which circumstances made necessary. Without their help and the facilities and efficiency of the OME our target could never have been met.

RICHARD WILBERFORCE (Chairman)
JOHN GARNETT
LAURANCE C. HUNTER

JEAN COLLINGRIDGE (Secretary)
D. R. BOWER (Assistant Secretary)

18 February 1972

Appendix 1: Summary of wage recommendations backdated to 1 November 1971

		Current minimum weekly rate £	Addition £	New minimum weekly rate £
Face workers	National Power Loading Agreement	30.00		34.50
	Third Daywage Structure:			
	Grade A	30.00	4.50	34.50
	B	24.92½		29.42½
	C	23.20		27.70
Other underground workers	1955 Daywage Structure:			
	Craftsmen	19.40	6.00	25.40
	Non-craftsmen	19.00		25.00
Surface workers	Craftsmen	18.35	5.00	23.35
	Non-craftsmen	18.00		23.00

The period covered by these recommendations is 1 November 1971 to 28 February 1973.

Appendix 2: Financial background

56. The NCB, operating within the limits of its financial constraints, made a number of offers for wage increases during the recent negotiations, the total cost of which, on the Board's calculation, would have been as follows:

Offer of 12 October 1971 £25 million per year
Offer of 13 December 1971 £28 million per year
Offer of 5 January 1972 £32 million per year
Offer of 10 February 1972 £52 million per year

The claim originally made by the NUM would have costed about £120 million per year, a later claim about £100 million per year.

These estimates include the addition to the wage bill incurred on account of other classes of workers whose pay is traditionally related to the main settlement.

57. In framing the initial offer of October 1971, the NCB had in mind the circumstances of the current financial year (1971–2) and that of the next year (1972–3), in which effects of the settlement would also be felt. The first figure of £25 million was determined in view of assessments of the demand for coal, productivity and inflationary expectations; the figure was subsequently raised to £32 million on the ground that productivity might be raised by 2 cwt a shift (i.e. between 4–5 per cent) – rather more than had first been considered likely. According to the NCB, the final offer, costing £52 million, could not be self-financed by forecast productivity-improvements as could the Board's previous offers. The additional costs of meeting such an increase would have required further improvements in the Board's financial results, which might come from the following sources: increased production and sales, yet further improved productivity, more effective cost control, and higher realization on products through either price increases or better quality control. On none of these scores could the prospect be said to be encouraging. Doubts existed about the market for extra output if it could be achieved; productivity-improvement estimates had already been stretched; cost control was already stringent; and the price increases of the last year had already threatened the competitiveness of coal relative to other fuels in important markets. The NCB then, was already at its limit, if not beyond it.

58. It is relevant here to consider two points made by the NUM with respect to the financing of their claim. First, it was argued that since the partial capital reconstruction of 1965–6 a large number of pits had closed, and that interest payments on debts attributable to these closures were a deadweight on the industry. Secondly, the anticipation of future closures meant accelerated depreciation of assets in collieries at risk, with the effect that the industry was bearing the costs of the future as well as those of the past. The conclusion drawn was that a capital reconstruction and a write-off of debt was now necessary to present a realistic financial position for the industry. Such a procedure would eliminate the need to achieve a surplus of £100

million a year to finance debt and depreciation which stood as a prior charge on the accounts before a 'true' surplus became available for the financing of wage increases. Neither of the NUM's points appears to be quite a true reflection of affairs, however. No pit has closed since 1965–6, the cost of which was not anticipated in the reconstruction of that year; and depreciation is calculated on a straight-line basis with no anticipation of future closures. Certainly not more than £35 million could become available on a continuing basis by a write-off of debt, and we return later to the question of a change in financial structure.

59. In our exploration of the consequences of the present strike, together with earlier disruptions to production in 1970 and 1971, it became clear that in any event the NCB is going to require some special assistance from government. Quite apart from the cost of a wage settlement, the deficit at the end of 1971–72 is likely to be well over £100 million, and on the basis of the NCB's last offer, offset by some nominal price rises, the deficit for 1972–3 could reach £125 million (NCB estimate). Thus some action to write down or write-off capital seems inevitable.

60. While recent events have highlighted and aggravated the financial difficulties of the NCB they have never been far below the surface in the last few years. Like other nationalized industries, the coal industry has statutory obligations and in addition is governed by the setting of a financial objective by the Treasury. According to the Coal Industry Nationalization Act of 1946,

the revenues of the Board shall not be less than sufficient for meeting all their outgoing properly chargeable to revenue account on an average of good and bad years.

The 1961 White Paper on the Financial and Economic Obligations of the Nationalized Industries (Cmnd 1337) required surpluses to be sufficient to cover deficits on revenue account over a period of five years. Provision was to be made from revenue to cover the difference between depreciation at historic cost and at replacement cost. And contributions were to be made to the general reserve. However, the NCB in fact now seeks to balance revenue year by year, but substantial deficits in 1965–6 and 1968–69 have by no means been balanced by the small surpluses achieved in other years. The NCB has been unable to make provision for renewal of assets at replacement cost. No provision for reserve has been made. The NCB was given a financial objective for the five-year period commencing 1963, namely to set aside £10 million a year towards the increased cost of the replacement of fixed assets. This objective extended to the year 1969–70, since when the objective has been to break even each year. On only one occasion, in 1963–4, was any sum set aside for this purpose of replacing fixed assets (£12·5 million). It appears that the NCB has been operating since the early 1960s without meeting the objectives set for it by the Government. In addition, cross-subsidization from open-cast mining and ancillary activities towards the normal mining operations has been regular practice, with the effect that the true costs of these latter operations must have been distorted. The NCB is clearly aware of the problems and has been discussing with the Government alternative methods of approach to what are evidently difficult, long-standing issues.

61. Our concern here cannot be to make recommendations on these wider problems, but it is important that these factors should be brought to light since they bear on the issues before us in an important way. An industry in the financial plight of the mining industry, unable to meet its obligations yet just managing from year to year without intervention, was certain to find it difficult to meet a substantial increase in wages, however justified that might be. In stretching its offer to a package costing over £50 million a year it had almost certainly already gone beyond what it could afford. The financial circumstances which constrained the Board were somewhat artificial, a fact recognized by Sir John Eden when he said it was

common knowledge that the whole question of the Board's financial structure has been in the air for some time, and obviously we shall have to give careful thought to the prospects of viability now before it (*Hansard*, 8 February 1972, col. 1263).

The NCB, in our view, went as far as it could in the light of its financial prospects, but its offers were based on an admittedly unsatisfactory financial structure that was ripe for change. In these circumstances the risk was inevitably run that the workforce of the industry would be asked to bear some of the cost of this structure in the form of a lower increase in wages than might be deemed justified on other grounds. We believe that this risk became a reality in the negotiations of late 1971, and we have set out the reasons why a higher wage increase is justified.

62. In making our recommendations for a higher rate of settlement than that finally offered by the Board we are aware of the possible consequences for the coal industry. The extent to which the added cost to the wage and salary bill consequent on these recommendations will have to be reflected in increased prices depends particularly on the rate at which productivity increases can be won to offset the effects of higher wage costs, on the extent to which cost effectiveness can be improved, and on the precise details of the reappraisal of the Board's financial structure which must now come. We cannot ignore the consequences of price increases for the product demand facing the industry, and we have been advised that while the future relationships among the prices of competing fuels cannot be accurately forecast, it is likely that any more than a marginal adjustment of coal prices would lead to a reduction in demand. This in time would imply a contraction of production and further loss of employment, whereas the Board's strategy has been to stabilize output at a level of 130 to 140 million tons a year. We appreciate the desire of those in the industry to achieve stability after so many years of decline, and we appreciate the benefits for those employed in the industry that stability would bring. But there does not appear to be any special magic in the range 130 to 140 million tons, and indeed contraction below that size, if it must come, would result in closure of the least efficient collieries and greater concentration on those operating at a profit. We recognize the social and economic costs of closure, especially for the peripheral regions of the country in which unemployment is already high. Nevertheless, if the Government wishes to maintain employment in these areas and in the coalmining industry in particular, the specific costs of so doing should be identified and made plain. The cost of subsidizing employment should not be reflected in a relative depression of the wages of those who work in the industry.

63. Clearly we must now expect that the promised review of the industry's finances will shortly come about. Our recommendations on the wage issue cannot anticipate that review but we

would expect that the costs of a once-for-all adjustment in the mining wage structure, to what we regard as a more appropriate position in the national pay structure, will be taken into account during any reappraisal.

Editorial Note on Statistical Problems Involved in Miners' Pay Comparisons

Until 1968 the only regular data on average earnings of manual workers were the Enquiries conducted by the Ministry of Labour in April and October each year. In September 1968 the first New Earnings Survey was introduced by the Department of Employment and Productivity (now the Department of Employment). Average earnings figures from the 1967 Enquiry and the 1971 New Earnings Survey (including those whose pay was affected by absence) were presented by the NUM as evidence of a significant alteration in the ratio between average earnings in coalmining as opposed to average earnings in 'all manufacturing industries'.

There was some discussion before the Court of Inquiry of the problems of non-comparability between the earnings Enquiry figures and the more recent New Earnings Survey figures for average earnings. Neither the NUM's submission nor the Court's Report could fully overcome the problems involved in using these series. We therefore think it necessary to describe here in some detail the two major difficulties involved.

Foremen and under-officials

The first major distinction between the two series is that Enquiry figures for average earnings reflect the inclusion of foremen and, in the case of coalmining, 'under-officials'. By contrast, the New Earnings Survey provides, for the first time, average earnings figures for just those workers in coalmining covered by the collective agreement between the NCB and the NUM.

This is an important consideration when Enquiry figures are used to establish changes in average earnings in coalmining over a period of time, for two reasons:

1. Average earnings of under-officials are clearly higher than for the other manual grades (the more so since piecework earnings have been eliminated at the face, etc.).

2. There is a high and rising ratio of under-officials to other workers.

Indeed, in the light of this, it seems rather remarkable that the NCB, in its own published annual earnings statistics, made no attempt to separate out the NUM grades from the under-officials.

There are further problems involved in attempting to compare earnings in coalmining with those in manufacturing on the basis of Enquiry figures. First, the ratios of foremen to other manual workers are not necessarily the same in manufacturing as in mining; and, second, the pay differentials between foremen and other workers may also diverge.

This means that two distortions arise when Enquiry figures are used to measure increases in miners' pay over a period of time:

1. The level of earnings of those workers covered by the NCB-NUM agreement appears higher than it really is.

2. This element of distortion has increased as the ratio of under-officials to other workers has risen.

Holiday pay

A second difference between Enquiry and New Earnings Survey figures is that whereas the former includes provision for holidays with pay in arriving at average earnings for the pay-week in question, the New Earnings Survey figures exclude any such provision. This distinction helps to explain the difference between the Enquiry figure for miners' average earnings, and the significantly lower average provided by the New Earnings Survey.

It is surprising, however, that there is very little difference at all between the two series' figures for average earnings in 'all manufacturing industries'. This suggests either that some manufacturing employers were failing to include holiday-pay provision in previous Enquiries, or that some were continuing to include it for the New Earnings Survey, or possibly both. These two factors taken together (under-officials and holiday provision) explain why the NES figures quoted in the NUM evidence for 1971 are significantly lower than the estimated Enquiry figure quoted in the Wilberforce Report.

An examination of these kind of distinctions by the Department of Employment could be useful, especially if the degree of non-comparability could be identified, and guidance offered to those wishing to make use of the series. It would need a very careful review of the official series by the Department of Employment to establish the degree of non-comparability as between six-monthly recorded earnings figures for manufacturing and for mining, and as between those series and the NES earnings data. These problems both affect estimates of the relative deterioration of miners' earnings.

The complexity of the problems involved explains why the Court of Inquiry chose to use Enquiry figures throughout Table A of its Report, in order to indicate the relative deterioration in miners' pay. (The October 1971 data were unpublished, and not available to the trade-union side.) However, the series used in the Wilberforce Report involves some under-estimation of the relative deterioration of miners' earnings during the 1960s because it does not allow for the effect of a rising proportion of under-officials in the series (i.e. earnings for the NUM grades would not have risen as much as the index indicates). The Wilberforce series gives a far more misleading impression of the 1970–71 comparative earnings levels of workers in manufacturing and NUM members in mining.

The most exact comparison is that available from the NES; as we have seen there are major defects in the comparability of the previous earnings series. In 1970 the NES showed that average gross weekly earnings of men in coalmining (including those whose pay was affected by absence) were by then *£3 a week lower* than the 'all manufacturing industries' figure. Because of the serious depression in manufacturing in 1971, and consequent reduction in actual hours worked there, this 'gap' was just over £2 in the 1971 NES. It would appear reasonable to say that before the strike the situation was that under even semi-depressed levels of manufacturing industry operation (as in 1970), gross weekly earnings for men on a strictly comparable basis were £3 a week higher in manufacturing than in coalmining. By contrast the series used in the Wilberforce Report gives the impression that miners' earnings in 1970–71 were almost exactly equal to average earnings in manufacturing.

Consequently, the recent pay settlement is likely to have put miners' earnings – for the time being – slightly above average manufacturing earnings. The next NES Survey, for April 1972, might be expected to show average gross earnings for men in the NUM grades about £1 to £2 a week above the manufacturing average (approximately £33 in manufacturing, and £34 to £35 in mining). As the miners' pay increase operates until February 1973 this differential over manufacturing will disappear later in 1973. The miner has in fact been established very near the manufacturing average so far as earnings are concerned. The misleading impression conveyed by the Wilberforce Report is that he was already at the point and has been put substantially above manual pay in manufacturing.

The Negotiated Settlement
and the NUM Ballot

As a result of negotiations following the Wilberforce Report the National Executive Committee secured further concessions from the NCB, which with the wage increase awarded by the Court of Inquiry it recommended to the members for acceptance:

1. [For the wage offer see the Wilberforce Report, Appendix 1, page 139.]

2. Daywage and Third Structure men on personal rates to get the full increase appropriate to their grade, i.e. £6, £5 and £4.50. Piecework contracts to be renegotiated locally so as to produce increases in line with that awarded to face workers. Effective from 1 November 1971.

3. Corresponding increases for coke and by-product workers effective from 1 November 1971.

4. The Board agreed that consequential increases for WPIS and Canteen Workers to be negotiated later, but effective from 1 November 1971.

5. Clerical workers to receive the same increase as surface workers. Effective from 1 November 1971.

6. Juveniles of eighteen years and over to get the full adult increase from 1 November 1971. The adult wage to be given to those aged twenty years from resumption of work, twelve months later those aged nineteen years to get the adult rate, and twelve months after that the adult rate to be paid at age eighteen years.

7. Winding enginemen to get an extra 80p a week.

8. A new five-grade structure for lorry drivers ranging from £23 to £24.50.

9. Five extra individual holidays a year starting 1 May 1972 at times agreed with management.

10. The five-day week bonus to be consolidated in the shift rate from 1 June 1972, i.e. the weekly wage will then be divided by five instead of six, for the daily rate.

11. Immediate joint discussions on a productivity scheme with a view to agreement by the end of September 1972.

12. A national subsidized transport agreement to be completed by 1 May 1972.

Elections Department of the Electoral Reform Society

---

6 Chancel Street
Southwark
London SE1
25 February 1972

Confidential

General Secretary
National Union of Mineworkers
London NW1

Dear Mr Daly

National Ballot

We have completed our task in this matter and here is our report.

The total number of valid votes was 217,620

The percentage voting 'Yes' was no less than $96\frac{1}{2}$

Put another way, your members voted Yes in a proportion of more than 27 to 1.

The actual figures are   Yes   210,039

                         No   7,581

	For	Against
Yorkshire	43,980	2400
South Wales	22,332	1078
Nottinghamshire	26,724	712
Scotland	13,387	767
Durham	18,015	389
Officials and Staff	15,549	139
Midlands	12,238	365
Derbyshire	9476	385
Northumberland	8745	218
North West	8249	244
Durham Mechanics	5331	131
Group 2 (Scotland)	3601	205
Cokemen	4102	78
Power Group	3916	56
Leicestershire	2453	56
South Derbyshire	2385	28
Kent	1895	186
Northumberland Mechanics	2137	45
North Wales	1644	29
Cumberland	1246	17
Power Group 2	1198	20
Durham Enginemen	1054	10
Yorkshire Enginemen	382	23
Totals	210,039	7581

Yours sincerely
Frank Britton
(signed)

Afterword
John Hughes

Through its title this book sets out an assertion and a question.

The assertion is embodied in the general theme that runs through the reasoned tone and the careful order of the evidence. It is that there is a quality that we can identify as social justice, and that the main points of the miners' case should be justified and can be justified in those terms.

If this assertion is granted, there are two things that may be said. One is that the miners had been dragged into a position where they were forced to use their industrial strength to ensure a just assessment of their claim. Clearly, the Government thought it could handle the industrial action it precipitated, and clearly it miscalculated. The miners throughout had sought a reasoned response to their claim, and in their case to the Wilberforce Committee they used rational argument instead of the language of power and confrontation. It is important for the future of labour relations in Britain that the final act of the miners' strike was one in which the NUM won its case at the level of reasoning and justice. The Wilberforce Report is couched in these terms: 'we believe the mineworkers at this particular time have a just case for special treatment'.

The second point to make is this. We live in a deeply irrational society if only prolonged strikes and widespread industrial damage can ensure that the felt injustices which a group of workers experience are carefully considered and recognized. A society of that kind is dangerous if it succeeds in repression and dangerous if its repression breaks down. In other words, the real social costs of a recourse to power bargaining are frighteningly high; they are not to be measured only in terms of economic loss, but of the anger, frustration, and loss of positive cooperation among workers

if and when a repressive state imposes its will. A deliberate recourse to power bargaining by the state is none the less an exercise of force, of violence, for being cloaked in the trimmings of
public authority and for covering itself with empty phrases about
the national interest.

By contrast, however sceptical we may be as to the pursuit of
reasoned argument and the examination of value systems in
areas of industrial conflict, this is a road that may offer social
benefits. We may actually confront people – and not simply those
directly involved – with real questions of social responsibility
(and many people have been made to think harder about the distribution of income, about work and its rewards, in the light of
the miners' case).

But in what sense were the miners a special case? Now this
may mean two rather different things. It may mean that there
were features peculiar to the mining industry or the miners' work
that have no equivalent elsewhere. Perhaps one might give as
an example the differential for underground workers which had
been set at £1 a week nearly twenty years ago; the NUM
claimed and secured a doubling of that differential (which in fact
simply put its real value back to what it had been all those years
ago). One might mention too the fact that the miners' pay structure has largely chosen to recognize reward for shift work
through the level of basic pay – whereas in other industries
distinct shift payments are a major and growing element in
earnings.

But to ask whether the miners were a special case may mean
something different, and something of more general importance.
The miners may have been a 'special case' in that they represented a combination of a number of problems that are found more
generally in British industry. My own view is that this is the real
significance of the miners' case. The miners were 'special' in that
they represented in a cumulative and extreme form most of the
main problems of Britain's industrial-relations system, of public-
sector management, and of national economic management too.
If that is so, then a study of the main features of the miners' situation and the miners' case can provide important clues as to the
labour problem – the workers' aspirations – in Britain to day.
In studying the miners' case we bring under review the main

burdens under which men labour. In studying the miners' case we find illumined the points of pressure in our industrial society.

Even in the midst of their struggle, with all its tensions, the miners had some awareness of this wider reference, which comes through in important parts of their case and its presentation. But, of course, the degree of industrial, organizational, and to some extent cultural isolation of the miners has limited their consciousness of these general connections and comparisons.

It is necessary to demonstrate this argument by a critical review of the main issues of general significance in the miners' case.

Declining industries

This is a wider problem than it may seem at first sight, since the special difficulties may attach to an industry or occupation with a persistent reduction in its manpower requirements whether these reflect a market decline or a shift to more capital-intensive technology. Coal was caught with both. Taken together, large-scale colliery reconstructions and power loading of coal account for more of the manpower fall since 1958 than does the decline in coal sales. Textiles have experienced a similar pattern; so has steel, with a sharper decline still to come.

Caught in this situation, the trade union and the workers concerned seem presented with an invidious trade-off. This is the more sharply felt where (as in the industries just mentioned) there is a high concentration of employment in the one industry in particular localities or sub-regions. The market system presents a choice between greater insecurity and more rapid rates of redundancy, or the acceptance of a persistent relative decline in pay. What often develops is a mixture of both. And this may emerge despite (to some extent because of) high rates of productivity advance. The miners' case explains this context in chapter 1. If that is 'exceptional' experience, it is one shared by the workers and trade unions in textiles and steel (and the postal side of the Post Office is now moving into a similar situation).

Thus, the market mechanism penalizes the penalized. Workers who are more exposed than others to loss of expectations in promotion and jobs may see no compensation for this through relative improvement in pay – instead they lose out there too. The long-term impact of this in the case of the miners was immense if we look back over the twenty years from 1950 to 1970. Employment fell by 400,000 and over the same period average earnings of manual workers in other industries increased 25 per cent more than the earnings of miners.

The Wilberforce Report (see paragraphs 30 and 42) accepted the unreasonableness of holding down miners' wages, accepted the case for an exceptional increase, and then argued 'if it cannot be paid for out of the NCB's revenue account . . . we think that the public, through the Government, should accept the charge'. Now this may mean much or little. It might be the beginning of a commitment to a more carefully planned management of both industrial contraction and provision of employment alternatives. Or it might mean some partial and temporary easement through revenue subsidies and capital write-off, with the general problems slowly reasserting themselves later on.

The miners have not yet been taken off the horns of this 'declining industry' dilemma. The pay settlement is clear; the future context of economic and financial management for coal is not.

The rigidities of nationalized-industry accounts

The miners, caught in their 'declining industry' dilemma, found themselves faced with that masterpiece of inscrutable bureaucratic nonsense – nationalized-industry accounting. 'Ability to pay' is confined within what are declared to be a combination of statutory obligations and commitments to the Treasury to achieve previously decreed financial targets. The miners' case unravelled as much as possible of the mystery and illogicality in chapter 5, and this attracted extensive comment in the Wilberforce Report's Appendix 2. The same rigidities and sheer economic irrationality were a major element in the Post Office dispute in 1971, and were discussed by the Hardman Committee (of which the present writer was a member) which examined that dispute.

The main points to bear in mind are these. Many nationalized industries work in market situations of considerable risk and uncertainty. It is not just a matter of competition from substitutes, but also shifts in technology and tastes. In many cases, when their market situation was strong, and large surpluses could have been built up to self-finance future development, these industries were not allowed to earn such surpluses. It would have been economically rational to have had the coal industry in the first ten years after nationalization earning surpluses that could have totalled £2000 million – this was a point that Lawrence Daly emphasized during the strike – but they were not permitted to. More recently both steel and the Post Office have had proposed price increases cut in half, with the consequence that they moved into severe revenue deficits (in the Post Office this was one of the irrational elements leading into the 1971 strike; in the steel industry a later capital reconstruction compensated rather belatedly for the damage done).

If nationalized industries have not been able to build up surpluses they are driven into heavy borrowing. At this point the Treasury forces them into a wildly unsuitable capital-debt structure, borrowing at fixed interest rates which then become a prior charge on the future revenue accounts. The high interest rates of recent years, and the compulsion on these industries to borrow long (when new governmental techniques had pushed up long-term gilt-edged interest rates), have made this still more burdensome. Outside of steel and aviation, the Treasury is still bitterly resisting any greater flexibility (through so-called Exchequer Dividend Capital, a kind of public-sector version of risk-taking equity capital). It operates instead, at long intervals and only after the financial constraints have precipitated labour or other economic crises, by occasional and fairly arbitrary capital write-offs.

The coal industry had a modest capital write-off in 1965. By 1970 it was overdue for another one, and it is an open secret that one was being considered by the Labour Government just before it fought and lost the 1970 election. One can only suggest that it has suited successive governments to put off such a capital reconstruction because the result would have been that the subsequent accounts would have signalled to the NUM that there was now more room for 'ability to pay' to meet their claim for some share in rising productivity and proceeds. The top-heavy debt structure served to obscure the big advances the

Coal Board had been making in both productivity and proceeds (these are examined in chapter 4). The accounts always demonstrated that there was no surplus to share. One of the minor ironies of NCB accounts was that they never showed a revenue surplus of more than half a million pounds; the managers of the industry and politicians could then take credit for operating 'in the black', but there was nothing there for the NUM to seek to redistribute.

For some reason best known to itself, the NCB at the Wilberforce Inquiry suggested that the 1965 capital write-off had anticipated and provided for all colliery closures since then. (They were of course kicking into their own goal, since they too know the industry has long needed a further capital reconstruction and have been openly asking for it.) Unfortunately the Wilberforce Report (see its Appendix 2) was to some extent influenced by this.

The fact is that none of the energy-policy forecasts, either in 1965 or later, came anywhere near anticipating the steep decline in coal sales, or the pace and cumulative scale of pit closures that went with it. But operating surpluses were large enough to allow conventional depreciation provision to continue. Any major capital write-off both compensates for the past and makes some attempt to anticipate future requirements. The new reconstruction of the Steel Corporation's capital does precisely that. Certainly, the 1965 capital write-off for coal could not be said to have anticipated so much as to avoid the need for a further major reconstruction and write-off now. In the words of the Wilberforce Report, 'action to write down or write-off capital seems inevitable'. This will help in the short run to ease the economic problems of the mining industry. But the general problem of the crude and rigid approach to nationalized-industry accounts continues. It is seen at its worst in the more labour-intensive nationalized industries, not only because for them problems of financial and economic strategy may be most difficult in a period of rapid inflation, but also because there is a temptation to leave the capital structure in a top-heavy state to restrict the apparent bargaining room of the workers concerned.

Damage from an under-employed and inflationary economy

One can identify a number of industries that suffer more than others from being at the receiving end of the under-employed and at the same time inflationary economy that has characterized Britain in 1970–71. Thus, in such an economy the railway system finds its workload falling while its operating costs are forced up; the same is true of the Post Office.

The coal industry has been doubly damaged. Firstly, under-employment of industrial capacity leads to reduced demand for coal. If this loss of the momentum of growth is prolonged (and we need to remember that only one year since 1965 – namely 1968 – has shown a sizeable rate of economic growth) then the coal industry finds itself driven either into an even more rigid resistance to what it views simply as wage-cost increases or into contemplation of further closures. In other words, the problems of management indicated in the two previous sections (a long period of decline, and a rigid accounting framework) are made even worse by the addition of a generally deflated economic climate. Secondly, the cost inflation that has accompanied every period of cyclical 'stop' in the post-war British economy further undermines the long-run market position, since it pushes up the production costs of the home-based labour-intensive fuel industry as against imported alternatives.

Obviously this kind of experience is not peculiar to the coal industry. But this climate of inadequate demand and cost inflation certainly added to the tension over income distribution, and the tension has yet to be reduced by the break-out towards a strategy of sustained economic growth. The reflection of this in the coal dispute is to be seen in the NUM's evidence on the market position in chapter 6, and in the explanantion in chapter 7 of the contribution of pay de-escalation, or the notorious 'n − 1' approach to the norm, to the creation of unemployment during 1971. Clearly the Wilberforce Report was not able to resolve these problems, since it could not guarantee that the economy would from now on secure rapid growth; its uneasiness is evident in paragraph 62 of the Report. But at least its conclusion is un-mistakeable.

The cost of subsidizing employment should not be reflected in a relative depression of the wages of those who work in the industry.

That was written about coal. It may with even more truth be said that the way to pursue a policy aiming at limiting unemployment is not to secure the general depression of the real wages of those who work in industry.

Implications of reformed pay systems

Against the depressing background of decline, and boxed in by the constraints of NCB accounts, there was nevertheless, a major reform of pay systems going on in the 1960s inside the coal industry. The main effect of this was to remove most of the small-group incentive payments systems and to create a pay structure in which basic rates – together with overtime – largely determined earnings. The new system was in character close to a system of measured day work. In important ways this 'reform' had damaged the pay position of miners instead of improving it.

For one thing, the miners had accepted a fairly rapid rate of internal redistribution of pay which actually involved levelling down in many cases. The levelling down had been made more marked by agreements which involved groups of workers in some coalfields marking time in money pay while inflation accelerated. The Wilberforce Report concluded (paragraph 23), 'too much was asked of men as the price of the new wages structure'.

Besides this, the NCB continued to use the old standards of wage-rate comparison when arguing about pay increases – despite the enormous change in the relationship between rates and earnings even within the last three years. The section of the miners' case on 'Earnings and pay rates' (chapter 3) completely demolished the NCB's primitive 'league table' arguments, and these simply disappeared without trace. The amazing thing is that the NCB, having achieved so much in terms of a reformed pay structure, should have been so grudging in the rewards they offered.

As Lawrence Daly argued in his concluding remarks to Wilberforce:

In all logic, there should have been some reward for our active cooperation in going over to a reformed pay system. Instead, we were penalized.

This is hardly a good advertisement for the replacement of payment-by-results systems by measured task work in other industries.

The new pay system had two distinct consequences. It cut out the earnings 'drift' that comes from the deterioration of incentive pay systems, and it was much less prone to the local disputes that had troubled the industry. These considerations are no less important in industries such as engineering, and particularly motors, where similar shifts to controlled day-wage systems are in process. The general issue is therefore clear; if the workers in an industry cooperate in the upheaval of differentials, including regional differentials, this is a very positive contribution – to be rewarded, not penalized. The existence of one union dealing with one corporation made this possible but by no means easy. By contrast, in industries such as motors, the equivalent process – including the attempt to level up to the best regional rates – has still a doubtful outcome. The fact is that major reforms of pay systems are likely to appear expensive in the short run, except perhaps in the expansion phase of the trade cycle.

The miners' pay reform was also moving in a direction contrary to pay systems in other parts of the public sector. There (in sectors such as other public utilities, and local government) the resistance to improved basic rates, which is often crude and inappropriate when connected to an irrationally applied norm, has led to deliberate moves away from time rates to a variety of additional payments (shift rates, lead-in and lieu payments, incentive pay) to boost earnings opportunities faster than basic rates. Perhaps we should make up our minds whether we want public-sector pay to move towards the kind of rationalization achieved by the miners, or to move instead in the opposite direction of a deliberate creation of local incentive systems and plus rates. 'Reform' at the moment means remarkably different things in different industries and services in Britain.

Priority for the low-paid

The NUM case makes clearer than almost any other modern pay claim both the special problems associated with the idea of giving priority to the low-paid and the real opportunities to help the low-paid that must now be grasped.

First of all, the other manual workers in mining who make up the membership of the NUM have been prepared to come to the rescue of the low-paid by accepting – indeed, demanding – a succession of settlements that gave most (both in money terms and proportionately) to the lowest-paid. My rough estimate is that the differential in earnings between coal-face workers and other manual workers in mining has been halved in the last five or six years. Of course this may well represent the most that we can expect as a direct contribution to helping the low-paid through a change in differentials; here again, with one union and a growing egalitarianism and sense of solidarity, a major re-distribution was possible. (Notice that face workers in coalfields such as Nottinghamshire have accepted a double process of re-distribution in favour of more rapid advance for face workers in other lower-paid coalfields, and also in favour of lower-paid grades.)

The miners, in essence, were pointing to the contrast between the contribution they had sought to make and the rapid build-up of the tax burden on the low-paid. The same governments that asked for restraint in pay increases from low-paid workers have steadily curtailed their real income through taxes. Michael Meacher's evidence shows the sheer weight of this, and the difficulty low-paid workers have in escaping from the poverty trap. There is no doubt that the miners, in insisting on breaking out through sharply higher pay, have brought the whole question of governmental responsibility into the centre of argument over incomes. The 1972 Budget can be seen as a first response, not only in its boldness in going for growth but also in the priority it gives to lower taxation and higher real income for the low- paid.

The miners served notice that the low-paid worker – where he has effective trade unions to back him – will not wait indefinitely for real improvement. If the Government does not want the cost-inflationary consequences of a pay policy on behalf of the low-paid that is pursued through money-wage bargaining alone, then they must join in as allies through a more progressive fiscal policy. The miners could rightly claim that so far as redistribution within their pay grades was concerned they had been prepared to give quite as much priority to the low-paid as anyone else, probably more. It is not only in mining that higher-paid workers can speed the process of improving the real standard of the low-paid; but there are real limits to this process. The higher salaried groups can more effectively be made to contribute through a redirection of fiscal policy (but note that this is to ask the present Government exactly to reverse all its initial fiscal policies). And there are industries that are so generally low-paid (such as agriculture) that there is no room for redistribution in their ranks.

The miners, through their earlier pay policies and now through their settlement, have done more to pull their industry's low-paid out of the 'poverty trap' than anyone else. We should not under-estimate the impact of that, not only on the attitudes of other trade unions as to the limits of the possible, but also on political strategy and fiscal policy. At least the miners may have forced a halt to the concerted drive that the Conservative Government has so far made towards a society of greater in-equality – backed by greater repression.

Recognizing the special case

The clear logic of Professor Clegg's evidence in support of the miners (see chapter 11) is both positive as to the need for some agency in the British industrial-relations system able to handle 'special cases' and optimistic as to the outcome being capable of providing lasting improvements in pay where a special case can be made out. There is no doubt that we are here touching on a major unresolved problem. There have been several cases in recent years which, in various combinations, showed on the one hand high productivity and positive cooperation by the labour force, and on the other low levels of reward (sometimes together with job insecurity or outright closures). How are these pressures to be dealt with?

The argument for a serious attempt to give more attention to special cases may be put not just in terms of equity but also of economic management. If the discontented set the pace in push-ing on pay, and yet their special situation goes unrecognized, the outcome is likely to be cost inflationary, and the cost inflationary push to be perpetuated. Belated and reluctant recognition of the special case in the course of damaging industrial disputes is a strange way of providing a third-party exercise in rationality. It is rather reminiscent of Charles Lamb's story about how the Chinese discovered roast pork; eventually someone thought of a better way to produce it than to burn the house down. Do we have to suffer exceptional economic damage and loss as the price of an occasional Wilberforce Report?

That is not to say that we are clear yet what kind of agency is needed. The evident weakness of the traditional Court of Inquiry is its inability to follow through into a serious economic analysis and economic programming. Yet if a major readjustment (in pay, etc.) is required in a short to medium-run period, then the relevant economic adjustments are serious matters and need both expertise and studies in depth over a period of time. Right now, we seem to have succeeded in producing parts of the required answer but not the whole answer.

For instance, in the case of Upper Clyde (UCS) we have had (belatedly and after long-drawn-out dispute) an exercise in more rational economic analysis which develops a new economic basis on which work can continue; but it is much less clear that the industrial-relations requirements of the proposed employment have been thought through. Are UCS workers to win through on the principle of employment, only to be presented by crude demands for a future wage freeze or for rigid dispute procedures?

In the case of the miners, we have had belatedly an exercise in the rational analysis of pay and differentials, but it is much less clear that the economic requirements of the new pay deal have been thought through. Are miners to win the principle of equity in handling their pay only to be presented with a new degree of constraint in the employment on offer?

It is better to have half-way rationality than no rationality at all. But it would be better still to recognize the interconnection of industrial relations and economic programming – whether our special case comes into prominence out of pay grievance, or out of attempted plant closures in a heavily unemployed labour market.

The whole argument, then, is that the miners' situation had in it many of the main elements that trouble our industrial-relations system and our industrial and national economic management. It was exceptional not by being different. It was exceptional in bringing together so many of the critical and unresolved elements in modern British industrial affairs. This is why it deserves attention. The miner's working environment may be unfamiliar. But when we analyse his grievances and problems they are all too familiar.

Nor should we imagine that a swiftly convened Court of Inquiry, and a sudden conversion to a combination of equity and rational argument, provide a sufficiently authentic version of a solution to such cumulative problems. Nor does short-term collective bargaining of the traditional kind, with its limited horizons and its propensity to look back instead of forward.

The argument of this Afterword leads in the direction of more extensive social and economic planning. It is difficult to cope with even any single one of the six main headings that have been distinguished except through systematic analysis and a programme that must stretch over a period of time; it is even less likely that we can tackle such questions when they come at us in combination, with a cumulative weight, unless we are prepared to adapt our industrial-relations systems and our economic management to a wider and continuing process of planning for change.

At Ruskin College, we have a small Trade Union Research Unit that has become deeply engaged in the analysis of many different kinds of collective bargaining and industrial-relations problems. We have been led inexorably to the need for this combination of longer-term analysis and strategic planning, of continuing economic analysis in closer connection with bargaining objectives. In eighteen months we have been involved in motors, in chemicals, in textiles, in public services, in distribution, in the Post Office, in steel, and of course in mining. The strategic-planning need has been common to them all. And if we are to understand the case of the miners aright, we should not see the Wilberforce Report as the end of the exercise but rather as a point of departure – a break out towards a more rational and more human planning of industrial development, one that is not afraid to call upon the participation of organized labour. The miners have much more to fight for. And so have we all.

Acknowledgement

Permission to reproduce material included in chapter 10 is acknowledged to H. A. Turner, F. Wilkinson and I P C Magazines Ltd.